UNEASY FRIENDSHIP

France and the United States

JULES ARCHER

FOUR WINDS PRESS/NEW YORK

Designed by Constance Ftera

Published by Four Winds Press
A Division of Scholastic Magazines, Inc., New York, New York
Copyright © 1972 by Jules Archer
All rights reserved.
Printed in the United States of America
Library of Congress Catalogue Card Number: 70-182117
0987654321

YOUNG ADULT BOOKS BY JULES ARCHER

To our second daughter by marriage

Elizabeth Anne Archer

with warmest affection

Contents

Introduction

WE AMERICANS have been taught to believe, from our earliest years in the classroom, in the traditional ties of friendship between the United States and France. Those bonds were forged by our respective revolutions and by Franco-American alliances in two world wars. Yet during the crucial decade of the 1960's, we were perplexed when the French, under Charles de Gaulle, withdrew from our NATO alliance, negotiated independently with Red China and the Soviet Union, attacked the value of the American dollar, opposed our policies in Vietnam and the Middle East, and thwarted our aims in the Common Market.

If France were truly America's "traditional friend," why was her behavior toward us so hostile?

Modern quarrels with our exasperating friends, the French, actually reflect the characteristic ambivalence of Franco-American relations as they *really* have been ever since the first

1

Frenchman set foot on our shores. Differences in culture, religion, history, language, geography, ethics and technology have always made mutual understanding difficult.

This book traces the fascinating interplay of Franco-American relations as they have swung back and forth between enthusiastic camaraderie and chilly hostility.

If this book proves anything, it is that the persistent difficulty most French and Americans have in achieving a genuine understanding of each other points to the need for more exchanges between the political scholars, writers, sociologists and social psychologists, businessmen, economists, high school and college students, lawyers, scientists and legislators of both countries. Such cross-fertilization can do much to enlighten the French about Americans, and the Americans about the French.

The French might be less exasperating if we understood them better. And they might find us less irritating in turn, if they knew us better. Hopefully, this book will contribute a modest beginning from this side of the Atlantic toward that important goal.

The writer would like to acknowledge the generous co-operation of M. Alain Chaillous, Director, *Service de Presse et D' Information*, at the French Embassy in New York, and his assistant, Mme. Monique Polgar, while at the same time holding them free of responsibility for any facts or interpretations with which they may disagree.

Jules Archer

Pine Plains, N.Y.

These figures from the facade of the Paris Opéra are allegorical representations of dancing. The artist is Jean Baptiste Carpeaux, a noted sculptor and painter of the nineteenth century.

FRENCH CULTURAL SERVICES

1
Cross-Fertilization

THE German philosopher Schopenhauer once described the problem people have in getting along by comparing them to porcupines who huddle together for wintertime warmth, only to drive each other apart again in the spring with their quills. That porcupine-like relationship between the French and Americans is the focus of this book.

American opiniòns about the French often depended on the state of our international relations. Yet, despite the doubts and reservations about one another, the French and the Americans have had a long history of influencing each other's development.

During the eighteenth and nineteenth centuries, Americans were repelled by the interminable involvement of the French in wars, but irresistibly attracted to some of the more spectacular elements of French culture. America's social leaders borrowed from the court of Louis XIV concepts of elaborate gallantry, the dueling code to uphold one's "honor," gambling, the display of a devil-may-care disposition, and elegant dress to indicate fine taste. Their somewhat exaggerated imitation of the French aristocracy gave ordinary Americans the impression that the French were a frivolous, vain, fickle, insincere people, and not to be taken seriously. This notion persisted. Nevertheless, the help of the French during the American Revolution made them enormously popular. One Frenchman, Brissot de Warville, helpfully suggested that Americans drop English, the language of the tyrant, and adopt French, the tongue of their generous ally.

When the United States won independence and sought to break away from the English look of its buildings, towns and parks, American officials often imitated French architecture and landscaping. French architects created some of America's most beautiful colleges, churches and public buildings, and it was a Frenchman who designed Washington, D.C.

The rage for things French intensified with the outbreak of the French Revolution. It became fashionable to subscribe to French newspapers. In the American press, professors, merchants, fashion stylists and wine importers ran advertisements in French. American farmers, incidentally, owe a debt to the French for their help in developing American wines, as well as the culture of rice and indigo. By the turn of the nineteenth century, America's social and governmental leaders had established salons where the dances, and often the language, were French. Elegant American women behaved coquettishly in the French manner, and slavishly followed the changes of fashion from Paris.

The French fad in America went into sharp decline after the excesses of the French Revolution and the tyranny of Napoleon. At the same time, there was a rise of religious feeling in the United States. The French language became associated with atheism and anarchy, and fell into disfavor. Franco-American relations grew even chillier with the harassment of American shipping by the French navy.

But by the conclusion of the Napoleonic Wars, America no longer had anything to fear from France. The sea lanes were open again, and communication and travel between the countries improved. Once more the influence of Paris took hold of America's style-setters. By 1830, the fashionable, prosperous bourgeoisie who went to Paris came home with French clothes and a few Gallic phrases to sprinkle in conversation. High schools and colleges vied with each other to lure French teachers onto their faculties.

Huguenot (Protestant) refugees settled in the coastal cities as fencing-masters, dancing-masters, finishing school masters, fashion experts and wig designers, thereby becoming missionaries of the French cult. They were a highly versatile people, of necessity; many immigrants with upper-class backgrounds were forced to accept menial jobs to survive. One fencing-master's wife advertised that she taught French, gave embroidery lessons and also took in fine washing.

In New York State, where Huguenots had influenced the tone of society from the early 1700's, the American gentry sent their children to a Huguenot school in New Rochelle. Girls learned French, water-color painting, and how to enter a drawing-room. Boys learned French, and how to bow and develop gracious manners.

7

Not all Americans were happy about the dancing schools established by the French, however. One reader of the *Boston News-Letter* protested that the institution was "a formidable . . . Monster in this part of the World . . . a Licentious and Expensive diversion." He further deplored the French influence in creating a demand "for Musick, Balls and Assemblies like Children for their Bells and Rattles." As for the fads of French cooking and fashions, he warned darkly, "Our Extravagance in Apparel and Luxury at our Tables are hastening the ruin of our country."

But many Americans found their lives considerably brightened by the culture of the resourceful French Protestants. The Huguenots taught them how to strip and weave worn-out garments into bright carpets, and introduced them to *bouillon, omelettes, purées, mayonnaise, hors d'oeuvres, consommé* and other typical French dishes. American homes were made daintier and more attractive with graceful French draperies, mirrors, china and furniture.

The Gallic influence on American fashionable society and entertainment was reinforced by the influx of French aristocrats fleeing the 1789 Revolution. Visiting New York in 1832, Mrs. Frances Trollope, mother of British novelist Anthony Trollope wrote acidly, "If it were not for the peculiar manner of walking, which distinguishes all American women, Broadway might be taken for a French street where it was the fashion of very smart ladies to promenade." French emigré Napoleon Murat, who married a rich Baltimore woman, said scornfully of the New York bourgeoisie, "All who have made a voyage to Europe try to ape the exclusive manners . . . affect to value everything foreign, and consider America as a barbarous country, where nothing elegant has ever been invented."

At fashionable Saratoga, New York, young men about town were noted to excel in the wearing of "mustachios and other exotic fashions," as if they were native Frenchmen or had been away in France so long that they bore the ineradicable marks of that culture.

"I go to the dancing school twice a week," a young man named Jay Cooke wrote to his brother from St. Louis in 1836. "Picture to yourself your brother Jay in a spacious ball-room with a beautiful French brunette by his side, skipping along and having fine times, and dressed in a fine brown coat . . . with white silk vest, black cassimere pants, white silk stockings, fine pumps, white handkerchief and gloves, hair dressed . . . talking Parley Voo with the beautiful creatures."

By the 1840's stylish American ladies used nothing but French toiletries, and regarded all Frenchmen as wicked, frivolous and delightful. "See Paris and die" became a popular slogan.

But not all the Americans who went abroad were enthralled by the French they observed or met. "The manners of the French women in high life are highly polished—they are perfectly lady-like and well bred—but you would be surprised to hear how trifling is their conversation," the wife of novelist James Fenimore Cooper wrote home. "Their dress, their Mantuamaker, their Marchande de Mode, form the great subject."

An American visitor to Paris in 1847 wrote in the magazine *The Daguerreotype:* "A Frenchman, more than any other man, is dependent upon things without [outside] himself. . . . For his best enjoyment he must have a succession of factitious excite-

American women have always been quick to imitate French modes of dress. The three styles here were popular in the 1820s.

NEW YORK PUBLIC LIBRARY

ments. Out of this want Paris has grown to be the capital of the world for superficial amusements. . . . Paris is the Elysium of the idler, and for barren minds a Paradise."

The differences between Protestant America and Catholic France have nourished a persistent American suspicion of French morality, family life, religion and philosophy. This misgiving is strongest among those Americans who look with distrust on all things foreign, and weakest among Americans with a cosmopolitan, international outlook. Most Americans have never been taught enough French to enable them to read or speak the language. Their ideas and attitudes about the French have been derived principally—and often inaccurately —from more cultured Americans. It is through the influence of the latter than an appreciation of French culture—theater, painting, sculpture, architecture, music and literature—has become essential for the educated American.

The American middle class imitated the American leisure class, who in turn emulated the French aristocracy. The middle class adopted just enough of the French life style from the upper class to enjoy the pleasures of feeling avant garde, but stopped short of any extremes, thus allowing themselves to feel they were still "proper" Americans. This middle class has often been the bridge by which the ideas of French intellectual leaders have percolated down into our mass culture.

The intellectuals and scientists of two nations usually have more in common with each other than with their own respective countrymen, who often find their ideas beyond easy understanding. On this level the French and Americans have almost always maintained a mutually respectful and often intimate relationship. Great Americans like Thomas Jefferson and Benjamin Franklin were as highly regarded by their French friends as they were at home, and were equally fond of the French elite in turn.

The French who settled among us—and their descendants—have contributed immeasurably to our development as a nation and to American culture. Although only about 100,000 French-born Americans live in the United States today, many millions of American citizens are of French descent. Among their fore-bears are such celebrated names as Paul Revere, Gouverneur Morris, John Jay, Alexander Hamilton, John Charles Frémont and Dupont de Nemours. Many French names, moreover, were Anglicized, so that even President Franklin Delano Roosevelt had a French ancestor named Delano, originally "de la Noye."

The French influence in America is also reflected in the names of many of our cities, called by French settlers after their native *villes*—New Rochelle, N.Y. (La Rochelle); New Orleans (Orléans); Bayonne, N.J. (Bayonne); Vincennes, Indiana and Ohio (Vincennes); etc. Fifteen American towns are named "Paris," and an even larger number "Lafayette," in admiration for those two unique French contributions to civilization. Faneuil Hall, the cradle of liberty in Boston, was also named for a Frenchman.

Many landmarks in France, in turn, memorialize our historic international friendship. In Paris there are a Place des Etats-Unis, statues of George Washington and Tom Paine, a Benjamin Franklin Museum, a monument to American volunteers who died fighting for France in World War I and a Musée Franco-Américain.

Transplanted French families established two of our best educational institutions: Vassar College and the Juilliard School of Music. Writers of French descent include Oliver LaFarge, Longfellow, Whittier, and Thoreau. Among our leading musicians are Darius Milhaud the composer, Pierre Monteux the conductor and André Previn the pianist and composer.

Other French settlers who left their imprint on the American way have included the Bowdoins, who founded the Massachusetts Humane Society; the Tiffanys, world reknowned jewelers; the Du Ponts, whose industrial and research centers have given us cellophane, rayon, nylon and rubberized paint. Allen Du Mont invented devices that made TV and radar possible. Robert Le Tourneau built our first huge earth-moving machines. Dr. Alexis Carrel won a Nobel Prize for his discoveries in surgery.

For generations the intellectual stimulation of Paris for writers, artists, musicians and scientists has drawn Americans to France to admire, study, create. Among the earliest writers who went to Paris to live for a time were Washington Irving and James Fenimore Cooper. Robert Fulton was the first American scientist to do research in France; he was followed by Samuel Morse, and later the Wright brothers.

During the first four decades of this century, Paris had the greatest impact on America's artists and writers, attracting a large American colony on the Left Bank. In February 1913, the School of Paris held an art show at the New York Armory, organized by New York artists to introduce French cubism and other new art forms to the American public. It was the first exhibit in America of Matisse, Marcel Duchamp and Picasso. Profoundly affected, many American artists rushed to Paris while the baffled public reacted with hostility and ridicule. Within six months, half a dozen New York galleries were exhibiting paintings in the modern vein by American artists.

Young Americans who fled to France after World War I, like magazine editor Harold E. Stearns, felt that American institutions had become frozen molds, enforcing nineteenth century ideas of morals, culture and "the Stone Age in business." The interests of youth, in contrast, were art and revolution, and they sought kindred spirits in Paris. When discontented youth wrote to Stearns asking what they could do about the low intellectual level of post-war America, his reply was succinct: "Get out!"

Paris in the twenties was the center for the artistically adventurous of every country—Picasso, Juan Gris, Modigliani, Brancusi, Mondrian, Kandinsky, Diaghelev, Klee, Copland, Duchamp, Hemingway, Joyce, Stein and Pound. Paris was where everything new in the world of the arts had happened, or was about to happen.

American poet e. e. cummings found Paris a far more human city to work in than New York, which, he complained, had become so big it had reduced its citizens to spiritual pygmies. As for *les Parisiennes,* he reported them to be "the finest girls God ever allowed to pasture in the air of this fresh earth." He added happily, "The fact that I could scarcely understand their language seemed irrelevant."

During this time, Pennsylvania-born Gertrude Stein was doing with words what Picasso was doing with paint. She took her inspiration from the paintings of Picasso, Renoir and Matisse which lined the walls of her Paris studio. A literary experimentalist, she strongly influenced the Americans who flocked to her salon. They, in turn, influenced the direction of the arts in America.

One of the moving spirits of the American colony in Paris was novelist Henry Miller. His books, rejected as obscene by American publishers, were accepted in sophisticated Paris. "I was so desperately hungry . . . for human warmth and understanding, but also for inspiration and illumination," Miller wrote. "During the dark years in Paris all these needs were answered."

Even poverty, he felt, was a joy in Paris because he never felt isolated or lonely. Every colorful street in the city brought him new impressions, feelings and ideas which found their way into his books. He loved the hand-written menus of the cafés, the sardonic waitresses, the bicycle cops who patrolled in pairs, the patched carpets of cheap hotels, the expert techniques of the street-cleaners.

"One needs no artificial stimulation, in Paris, to create," Miller wrote. "The atmosphere is saturated with creation. One has to make an effort to avoid being overstimulated. . . . The whole street is given up to quiet, joyous work. Every house contains a writer, painter, musician, sculptor, dancer, or actor. It is such a quiet street and yet there is such activity going on silently. . . . This is how it is on my street but there are hundreds of such streets in Paris. There is a constant army of artists at work, the largest of any city in the world. This is what makes Paris, this vast group of men and women devoted to the things of the spirit."

In 1971, Houston, Texas, felt this breath of Paris when Mr. and Mrs. John de Ménil settled there and sought to re-create for Texans the impact of French chapels displaying paintings by Matisse and Léger. They erected a non-denominational chapel featuring abstract paintings. "So many . . .

The unique character of Parisian streets is evident in this photograph of the Rue Norvins in Montmartre, a section of the city that has always been popular with artists.

FRENCH CULTURAL SERVICES

girls come in and just sit, looking at the paintings," reported a guard. "When they get up to leave, they're crying. It's an intense experience."

The impact of American culture on France has also caused some French to weep, but not for the same reason. With the accelerated pace of Americanization after World War II, drugstores, juke boxes, American supermarkets and movies have robbed Paris of some of its exotic glamor. Floods of tourists and the 14,000 Americans living in Paris have diluted some of the Gallic atmosphere.

The American look has penetrated all levels of French life. The streets are crowded with cars, the stores are jammed with refrigerators and washing machines, and many French spend too many hours in front of their TV sets. Young French businessmen, hatless like their American counterparts, grab quick American lunches in self-service cafeterias. The common ailment of the average Frenchman, cirrhosis of the liver—from too much wine—now has new medical competition—"*les ulcers américains.*"

Tradition is still strong in the French countryside, but more and more the old look of France is being transformed by the emergence of superhighways, cloverleafs, whole new suburbs and cities springing up around the country, beefburger quicklunch spots, and young people in blue jeans and love beads.

Many French nationalists are distressed and criticize the United States as a mass production society which, by spreading material wealth among the masses, has lowered the standards of design and esthetics. "You Americans have more of everything than we have," declared one French journalist, "but it's all so bad, who would want it?"

Such views are usually second-hand. Unlike the American, the Frenchman seldom leaves his borders to investigate other countries personally. Thrift is one reason; another is that he really considers himself to be living in the best of all possible worlds, and cannot conceive of finding any more interesting life style abroad.

Nevertheless, tourism in the United States is increasing among the well-to-do French. From only 300 in 1961 the number jumped to 125,000 just six years later.

How do the French see us? Coming from a country which could easily fit within the borders of Texas, they are astonished by the size of the United States. An everyday air journey from New York to Los Angeles would be comparable to traveling from Paris to the Middle East for the average Frenchman. For him, everything in the United States seems on a gargantuan scale.

When Sorbonne sociologist Dr. Raymond Aron visited the United States, he was struck by the fact that Americans "speak of dollars, of price, more than anywhere else in the world. In France a suspension bridge would be singled out for the tourist's admiration by reason of its length, height, possibly the difficulties of construction and the genius of the architect; in San Francisco and elsewhere people rave about the sixty-million-dollar bridge."

He added, "A Frenchman who visits the United States cannot fail to be struck by certain facts: the style, which seems vulgar to him, of much of the radio and television, the sordidness of the sensational and scandal-oriented press, the provincialism of much of the news . . . the mediocrity of many of the films."

The French visitor to the United States is distressed by the "sameness" of so many Americans, and by the pressures for conformity. He is also suspicious of the stereotyped smiles of waitresses, service station attendants and salesgirls. He finds them impersonal and insincere, unlike their grumpier—but more candid—French counterparts.

Returning French travelers report that Amercian food is edible but tasteless: steaks handsome to look at but without flavor; soda fountain drinks diluted; strawberry shortcake greatly inferior to French strawberry tarts. They deplore the American emphasis on quantity instead of quality. Many were shocked by parents who let their daughters go dancing at thirteen and use make-up by fifteen.

What they liked best were our motels, our plumbing, our well-equipped transcontinental buses with wide windows, our eight-lane highways for fast travel, our tidy New England villages, the great sense of space, and the friendliness of the average American. Visiting French philosopher Jean-François Revel was greatly impressed with the idealism of American youth. He considered them greater catalysts for change than the youth of France, who did more talking than acting.

Both Frenchmen and Americans who visit each others' countries often make the mistake of comparing the best at home with the worst they encounter abroad. A Frenchman will deplore the vulgarity he finds in American TV and cheap magazines, while an American will turn up his nose at dirty French streets.

Recently, the torch of culture seems to have slipped somewhat from French hands. New French novels are not much read today outside of France. The School of Paris is now less the center of the art world than its offspring, the New York School. French drama and poetry do not make literary news as often. The French cultural genius today blazes brightest, perhaps, in the work of such poetic filmmakers as Jean Cocteau and the existentialist plays of Jean-Paul Sartre.

Perhaps the most essential difference between the French and the Americans is that the French, with a long history of invasions of their country as reminders, tend to be profoundly pessimistic and don't expect too much of human nature. The Americans, whose uninvaded land has grown from a handful of crude settlements to a nation of great technological achievements, tend to be generally optimistic.

Nevertheless, with so many bonds in common—military, political, agricultural, economic and artistic—to say nothing of dedication of the American fashion industry to Paris *couture*—it was inevitable that Franco-American friendship should persist over the centuries. But the basic differences between us have often led to noisy quarrels as we shall see when, with this general background in mind, we trace the whole story of our relations with our exasperating friends, the French.

2

The French Come to America

ONLY a dozen years after Columbus demonstrated that you wouldn't fall off the edge of the earth if you sailed west, French fishermen began trawling off the Grand Banks of Newfoundland, which British explorer John Cabot had described as "swarming with fish." Not until 1524, however, did French King Francis I decide to get into the international exploring race. He hoped to beat Italy, Spain and Portugal to the discovery of the still-elusive short passage to the wealth of the Indies, as eastern Asia was then called. Flying the French flag, Italian navigator Giovanni da Verrazano poked around what is now called the Hudson River, Narragansett Bay, Cape Cod, Maine, Nova Scotia and Newfoundland, but failed to find the isthmus that would bring him swift access to the beautiful silks of China. Francis I was nevertheless tempted a second time by rumors of gold, silver and ruby mines which the Spaniards were reported to have discovered in the New World.

The Pope had already granted Spain and Portugal the lands their explorers had discovered in the New World, but the French King had no intention of being excluded from the spoils.

"Show me," he challenged rival courts, "that clause in the will of 'Father Adam' which divides the earth between the Spanish and the Portuguese, and excludes the French."

Eager for his share of gold, silver and rubies, but wary of clashes overseas with Spanish power, Francis trickled $1,200 of his own silver livres into the hands of Jacques Cartier, a French mariner of St. Malo. Cartier made several exploratory voyages around Newfoundland between 1533 and 1543. He discovered the majestic St. Lawrence River, reaching Montreal (Royal Mountain) which he named.

He made friends with the Huron Indians while waiting for spring, when he would be able to return. Once they understood what he wanted, the Huron, who were gifted talespinners, told Cartier fascinating stories of a wonderful Kingdom of Saguenay where such mines were operated by one-legged white men who flew like bats and lived without eating.

Excited, Cartier took the Huron chief home to Paris to convince Francis, whose greed made him as gullible as the explorer. The king hastily outfitted a new ten-ship fleet, sent Cartier back to claim the mythical kindom for France, and instructed him to return weighed down with gold, silver and rubies for Francis's coffers.

The explorer did discover deposits of brass-yellow metal and gems that glittered like diamonds, and proudly brought

23

Jacques Cartier, a French navigator and explorer of the early sixteenth century, discovered the St. Lawrence River.

NEW YORK PUBLIC LIBRARY

home a shipload. Unhappily for poor Cartier, the "gold" proved to be iron pyrites—worthless "fool's gold"—and the "diamonds" were nothing but quartz crystals.

The first successful French settlements in the New World were unofficial—those made by fishermen at the Grand Banks. Needing land bases to cure (dry) their codfish with a minimum of salt, in order to preserve them in shipment, they established landfalls in Cape Breton and the Gaspé Peninsula. They found the Indians willing to barter valuable beaver furs, which were in great demand in Europe for coat collars and hats, for axes, trinkets, kettles and cloth. So the fishermen began to bring back trading goods from France to the St. Lawrence region. Trading posts sprang up at Quebec, Montreal, and Trois Rivières. Expeditions of fur traders pushed into unexplored Indian territory, gradually spreading French influence throughout the Great Lakes and Mississippi Valley regions.

At first, Catholic France was too torn by religious strife to attempt official colonization of the New World. Savage persecution of the Huguenots by King Henry II (1547–1559) kept France embroiled in civil war almost until the seventeenth century.

The first purposeful French efforts to establish colonies in North America were dismal failures. In February 1562, a group of thirty Huguenots left France to seek religious freedom abroad. They were dropped ashore in a South Carolina wilderness but they soon grew homesick. A flimsy vessel of logs, with shirts and bedclothes as sails, took them back into the Atlantic, where they almost perished. Fortunately, a passing British ship rescued them and brought them to London.

At the beginning of the seventeenth century, King Henry

IV—Henry of Navarre, France's first Bourbon ruler—decided to exploit Canada's fur trade. He granted monopolies to French companies willing to finance American settlements. Between 1603 and 1615 explorer Samuel de Champlain made eleven voyages to eastern Canada for one of these companies.

He helped found Quebec, the first permanent French colony in America, as well as Port Royal in Nova Scotia. Strengthening French relations with the Huron Indians, Champlain helped them drive the hostile Iroquois out of the St. Lawrence valley. In an oar-driven small schooner, he also explored the coast of New England as far south as Cap Cod.

A few French companies persisted in the search for the elusive passage to the Orient. One Frenchman, sent to explore the Green Bay area in the late 1630's, optimistically took along a ceremonial robe of embroidered Chinese damask to wear at his official reception in Peking.

The French were successful in winning control of the Canadian fur trade primarily because of the skillful work of their Jesuit missionary-explorers among the Huron, who daringly pushed into wilderness territory, enduring cold and hunger to discover new lands and new Indian souls to save. They apparently had little fear of the torture or death they risked should they be captured by hostile Iroquois, who were the best organized and most powerful of all the Eastern Indians, and who controlled upper New York State. "The joy one feels," explained one Jesuit, "when one has baptized a savage, who dies shortly after and flies straight to heaven to become an angel, is a joy that surpasses all imagination."

The missionaries worked together with the French fur traders partly in order to survive, partly to keep that area of

*Samuel de Champlain made numerous voyages to eastern Can-
ada for a French fur trading company during the early 1600s
and helped to establish the French settlement of Quebec.*

NEW YORK PUBLIC LIBRARY

the New World both French and Catholic. Except for the Iroquois, the French got along better with the Indians than either the British or Dutch did. More sophisticated and less prejudiced, they freely intermarried, learned Indian languages and customs, and did not hesitate to live among the tribes and adopt their ways.

Young King Louis XIV, taking over France from his regents in 1661, decided to develop "New France" (Canada) as a royal province. He sent out fresh shiploads of colonists, most of them prisoners or shanghaied Frenchmen who were terrified by the prospect of life among "bloodthirsty savages." And when Count Louis de Frontenac became Governor of Quebec in 1672, his ten-year term was marked by a vigorous westward expansion to Lake Michigan. A chain of forts, trading stations and missions was left in the wake of his explorers, in keeping with the current French policy.

While the British cemented their hold on the American coast from Maine to Georgia, Frontenac explored the West. From Lake Michigan he sent a canoe expedition consisting of the successful fur trader, Louis Joliet, and the adventurous French missionary, Father Jacques Marquette, to explore the tributaries of the Mississippi. They drifted south on the great stream the Indians called "the Father of Waters" to the mouth of the Arkansas, almost to the northern border of what is now Louisiana. When friendly Indians warned that tribes further south were hostile and dangerous, they turned back to Mackinaw.

Frontenac realized the strategic importance of the Mississippi—it was at the back door of the English and the doorstep of the Spanish. He urged Louis XIV to send an expedition

Father Jacques Marquette, a French missionary, and the fur trader Louis Joliet were sent by the Governor of Quebec to explore the Mississippi River and its tributaries. Here they gaze upon this great river, which the Indians called "the Father of Waters."

NEW YORK PUBLIC LIBRARY

Robert de La Salle was commissioned by French King Louis XIV to fortify the Mississippi Valley against encroachments by the Spanish and British. Here he is seen landing in Matagorda Bay in what is now southeastern Texas.

NEW YORK PUBLIC LIBRARY

to build forts along the Mississippi Valley to control it for France. His emissary to the King, explorer Robert de La Salle, succeeded in winning this mission for himself.

In 1697, with the help of Indians, La Salle built a fort at the site of Peoria, Illinois. When he ran out of supplies, La Salle returned to Canada on foot, a thousand miles through the snow. He found the fort deserted and in ruins, but continued south along the Mississippi, building new forts in regions no European had ever explored.

Finally reaching the Gulf of Mexico in 1682, he planted the white banner of the Bourbons, claiming all the land drained by the Mississippi for Louis XIV as "Louisiana." He continued fortifying this territory, twice as large as France, Spain and Germany combined, against the British.

La Salle had to return to France to refute charges that his expedition down the Mississippi had been "wholly useless." But by the time he arrived in Paris, France was at war with Spain, and Louis XIV now saw a military value to the Louisiana territory.

He sent La Salle back with four ships and a company of soldiers to establish a fort at the mouth of the Mississippi and harass the Spanish in Florida and Mexico. Named "Viceroy of North America," La Salle was the only Frenchman ever to be appointed ruler of what later became the United States.

When he returned to the Gulf of Mexico, however, he was unable to find the mouth of the Mississippi and landed in Texas instead. Surviving on buffalo food provided by friendly Indians, he and his men built a fort where Galveston and Corpus Christi now stand. La Salle sought to reach Canada on foot in order to get more supplies for the settlement. But the seventeen-man detachment he led mutinied, and he was assassinated soon after leaving the fort.

Even before his ill-fated return to America, however, La Salle had changed the balance of power in the New World. Britain found herself threatened by a strategically-placed chain of forts that threatened the rear of her colonies and barred the way to colonial expansion. British fur traders also resented the French trading posts strung from Canada to the Gulf of Mexico. They were angered by France's claim to exclusive rights of navigation on the Mississippi, which the French called the Messachabé, a Gallic rendering of its Indian name.

Further resentment of Catholic France was inflamed by Huguenot refugees who fled to America with horrendous tales of persecution in their homeland. In October 1685, Louis XIV had issued the anti-Protestant Edict of Nantes, which sent hundreds of thousands of French Huguenots fleeing abroad for asylum.

"The blood-soaked soil of France cries to heaven for vengeance," declaimed refugee Solomon Legaré from America. "France, guilty France, will never be blest with peace, prosperity and quiet; but on the contrary, trouble, violence and revolution after revolution will vex and rend those who have thus troubled and murdered the people of God." He urged his children never to think of returning to France "if you would keep clear of the fearful curse which hangs over it!"

The Huguenot settlers brought with them the arts, accomplishments and graces of the most polished civilization of that day, together with a French gaiety and good humor that contrasted sharply with puritanical New England and Pennsylvania sobriety. Their contagious introduction of a light touch to colonial life—including cheerful colors, fabrics and charming furnishings—gradually made the everyday existence of many Americans considerably brighter.

A major clash between Protestant Britain and Catholic France in America was inevitable, not only because of religious conflict, but also because both powers were competing for power and trade in every part of the world. Their struggle in America, breaking out in 1689, lasted seventy years.

This conflict included King William's War (1689–1697), Queen Anne's War (1702–1713), and King George's War (1744–1748).

Although Louis XIV lost Queen Anne's War, he left an enduring memorial in his patronage of the arts in France. Under Louis, French society had become the most cultured and sophisticated in the world. The glorious palace at Versailles, and such brilliant writers as Molière, Racine, Corneille, Rochefoucauld and Fontaine, were characteristic of a flowering seventeenth century civilization.

From his elegant pinnacle at Versailles, Louis had viewed America simply as a primitive land useful as a source of minerals, furs and tobacco, but fit only for Indians, coarse traders, fanatical missionaries, the hoi polloi and Huguenots. Canada, Voltaire scoffed, was only "a few acres of snow." Whenever it was necessary to send settlers to colonize French holdings, Louis ordered the jails and hospitals scoured for candidates. Incorrigible family black sheep, soldiers, paupers, prostitutes, political rebels and unwary peasants were kidnapped and shipped under guard to the colonies. Some gullible freemen were induced to join the shanghaied victims by rosy promises of free land, indolent ease and instant wealth. ("The French

33

never leave France," French film director Jean Aurel once explained, "because they think no place could be better. . . . Only the worst Frenchmen leave France. . . . We sent our worst to the colonies.")

When Louis XIV died, the French treasury was almost empty. The regents ruling for his small son, Louis XV, turned over fund-raising to a shrewd Scottish promoter named John Law. He created the Mississippi Company and sold stock to credulous French investors eager to exploit the fabled riches of the Louisiana territory, which was said to contain pearl fisheries, and gold and silver mines.

Law's plan called for sending 6,000 settlers to reap this harvest, with 3,000 black slaves doing the hard work. The first volunteer colonists, some 300 in number, arrived in June 1718 and fanned out up the Mississippi. About 400 soldiers and convicts who came with them were kept in New Orleans by French explorer Jean Baptiste de Bienville, who had founded the town and was now Governor of the territory.

But when gold, silver and pearls failed to materialize, disillusionment spread swiftly through the settlement. Bienville discovered he could not control the disgusted colonists or persuade them to work. Most spent their time drinking, fighting, and trying to steal enough money to leave. Bienville sought, unsuccessfully, to enslave the Indians for labor, and was forced to pay for slaves imported from the West Indies.

Despite John Law's attempt to keep the colony solvent by flooding it with worthless paper money, the Mississippi Company went bankrupt. Bienville tried to save the Louisiana settlements by urging colonists to grow their own food.

"I neglect nothing to turn the attention of the inhabitants

34

The dramas of Molière are a product of the creative activity that flourished in seventeenth century France, during the reign of Louis XIV. Here are members of the French troupe La Comédie Française in a scene from "Les Fourberies de Scapin" ("The Rogueries of Scapin").

FRENCH CULTURAL SERVICES

to agricultural pursuits," he complained to Louis XV, "but in general they are worthless, lazy, dissolute, and most of them recoil from the labors necessary to improve the lands." To make matters worse, the settlements were constantly attacked by Chickasaw Indians, who resented the French invasion of their lands. To fight them, Bienville had only troops he derided as "pitiful blackguards."

"There are but one or two men among them whose size is above five feet," he protested to the King, "and as to the rest, they are under four feet and ten inches. . . . More than one-half have already been whipped for larceny. In a word, these useless beings are not worth the food bestowed upon them." It was obvious that King Louis was keeping his tallest soldiers in France to impress more important enemies.

Bienville's cup of humiliation ran over when the Chickasaw defeated his undersized troops. Unable to make French colonialism work because of the shortsighted and greedy policies of the Colonial Department in Paris, he gave up and left the colony in 1743. Bienville's discouraging experience with Louisiana may well have influenced the history-minded Napoleon, who decided sixty years later to swap the "worthless" territory with Jefferson for $14 million in hard cash.

3

Guerrilla Warfare— French and Indian Style

IN 1744 Europe erupted in another of the interminable wars that involved France and England on opposite sides. In America it was known as King George's War.

William Pepperell, a merchant of Kittery, Maine, conceived a daring scheme to help his motherland. Leading an expedition of 4,000 Yankee farmers and fishermen, he invaded Cape Breton Island in an attempt to capture the great 150-gun, 30-foot high stone Louisbourg fortress that Louis XV had erected at a cost of $10 million.

The fortress was vital to the French because it protected the harbor that guarded the entrance to their settlements along the St. Lawrence, and sheltered their fishing, merchant and naval fleets. And the New Englanders had an extra reason for wanting to take it: Louisbourg also sheltered French privateers that had plundered Massachusetts fishing vessels.

Benjamin Franklin had scoffed at the plan to seize the fortress as "far too hard a nut for their teeth to crack." But the Royal Navy agreed to land Pepperell and his men on a beachhead a few miles from Louisbourg. The invaders attacked a French battery on the perimeter. They captured its artillery and dragged it through swampland to open fire upon the astonished defenders of the fort.

When the French guns thundered a reply, the irrepressible New Englanders chased after their cannonballs and returned them to the fort via well-placed artillery fire. They provided themselves with food for the six weeks of their siege by fishing while the British fleet stood offshore to prevent the French Navy from coming to the rescue of the defenders. The fort's demoralized commander finally hoisted the white flag.

The news was received in Boston with an astonishment matched in England, where a delighted King George II made Pepperell a baronet. The jubilant New Englanders occupied their fort, waiting for British troops to relieve them. But none came. A quarter of the force died of disease and malnutrition during the rugged winter of 1745–46. Relief came in the spring only after their angry officers warned London of imminent mutiny.

To the dismay of the American conquerors of Louisbourg, King George II handed that fortress back to the French under a territorial swap in the 1748 Treaty of Aix-la-Chapelle. New Englanders began to mutter about the futility of fighting for a King whose trades for the advantage of Britain were to the disadvantage of British colonists in the New World. They were nevertheless filled with a new confidence in their own ability to teach a powerful nation of the Old World respect for their fighting ability. Cocky defiance, fueled by growing resentment over colonial grievances, began to characterize their attitude toward Britain as well.

By 1750, only 80,000 Frenchmen had been shanghaied or induced to settle all the colonies of New France, compared to over a million Englishmen who had flocked to the Atlantic seaboard. There were a number of reasons for this.

France insisted upon governing its provinces from Paris, whereas King George II made his American colonies more attractive to settlers by allowing them relatively more self-rule. France allowed only Catholics in her colonies; emigrating Huguenots were forced to settle in other countries of Europe or in the British or Dutch parts of America. Farmers, the largest occupational group in France, received no inducement to settle New France because the French concentrated on exploiting only the fur and fish resources of America. Most French, moreover, were more reluctant to emigrate than the British.

At the end of King George's War, Britain claimed that her control of Nova Scotia entitled her to the adjacent territories of New Brunswick and the Gaspé Peninsula. France objected, pointing out that the only settlement in Nova Scotia was French, with some 7,000 Acadians living on both sides of the Bay of Fundy. So Britain sent 2,500 settlers to the east coast to establish the British town of Halifax.

As new stresses and strains developed between England and France, the two Nova Scotia colonies became increasingly antagonistic. France sent secret agents to the Acadians to urge them to remain loyal to King Louis XV, promising that he would soon reconquer Nova Scotia for France.

English fur traders from Pennsylvania and Virginia, meanwhile, began pushing into the Ohio Valley and bribing the Indians there away from their French alliances. Enraged French fur traders attacked the British posts, and hastened the establishment of their own trading posts in the region. In 1749, the Governor General of New France accused the British traders of trespassing on King Louis's lands, and sent troops into the valley to drive them back east of the Appalachians.

The worried governor of Virginia, Robert Dinwiddie, dispatched a twenty-one-year-old surveyor named George Washington on a dangerous journey up the Ohio Valley to several French forts. Ostensibly sent to deliver a British protest, he was actually sent to reconnoiter.

The trip proved an arduous one. On his way back from Fort Le Boeuf, the young Virginian was almost drowned when he fell off his raft into the icy Allegheny River. He was also shot at by an Indian who was only fifty feet away but whose aim was miserable. Reporting these tribulations to the Scottish Dinwiddie—who called him a "braw laddie"—Washington warned that the French were determined to occupy the entire Ohio territory.

America now stood on the brink of the most crucial of all the early wars to decide whether France or England would become the primary power in the New World: the French and Indian War (1754–1763). This time hostilities began in North America itself, without any declaration of war. The conflict deepened two years later when the Seven Years' War broke out in Europe. But King George II had already committed his best forces to the expulsion of the French from their American forts.

The French traders in the Ohio Valley, equally determined

not to be driven out, declared war on every English-speaking trader or settler in the region. Outnumbered fifteen to one, the French resorted to guerrilla tactics, and with their Indian allies they set ambushes and fought from behind trees against British troops marching in ranks.

The French enjoyed territorial advantages. The two chief rivers of America, the St. Lawrence and the Mississippi, were under their control. They also now had a chain of sixty forts from Quebec to the Gulf of Mexico on sites which later developed into the cities of Detroit, Chicago, St. Louis, Natchez and New Orleans, among others.

With Washington as his aide-de-camp, General Edward Braddock led British troops with American and Indian auxiliaries against Fort Duquesne. As they marched in formation through a ravine they were ambushed by Indian allies of the French. The troops, Washington recorded later, "broke and ran as sheep pursued by dogs," abandoning all their equipment. The Indians killed or wounded two-thirds of the British forces and fatally wounded Braddock. This "Battle of the Wilderness" on July 9, 1755, ended with a dismal but skillful retreat led by Washington.

The jubilant French quickly seized two forts in upstate New York and beat off a British attempt to retake Forts Louisbourg and Ticonderoga. Thousands of frontier families fled from the French and Indians in panic.

William Pitt, the British Prime Minister, realized grimly that the whole balance of British power lay in the outcome of the struggle in the colonies. He threw all of England's resources into defeating the French in the New World. Reinforcements were rushed to America under the leadership of such expert generals as Wolfe, Amherst and Forbes. The tide began to turn.

Young General James Wolfe, advancing on Quebec in 1759, was warned by senior generals to retreat from the St. Lawrence before his forces were frozen in for the winter. Instead, he proposed scaling the steep cliffs south of Quebec at night to storm the fortress on the heights called "the Gibralter of America." His staff said the plan was impossible.

"Gentlemen," Wolfe replied, "since you are all so sure that it cannot be done, the enemy will also think so, and it will not occur to him that we would undertake it. Accordingly we shall scale the cliffs tonight!"

French General Montcalm de Saint-Véran was caught by surprise. Both he and Wolfe died in a fierce battle fought on the Plains of Abraham, and the French lost control of Quebec. The British conquest of Canada was completed with Amherst's capture of Montreal. France had lost its North American empire, and her 60,000 colonists fell under British rule. This defeat for France was hailed by Voltaire, France's controversial dissenter, as "a triumph of liberalism over despotism."

But the British conquerors had shown that they, too, could be despotic, rivalling France's cruelty in expelling some 400,000 Huguenots. When British Colonel Charles Lawrence took over Acadia (Nova Scotia) as Governor, he was incensed by the refusal of some 7,000 French Acadians to swear an oath of loyalty to the British crown. In September, 1755, he ordered them deported. In a chaotic atmosphere of haste and confusion, during which families and friends were separated, five British vessels took the Acadians to the American colonies. Their villages were burned to the ground behind them. About a thousand escaped to the woods, some fleeing to France, others to Louisiana or Canada. Most of those deported were forced to labor for Huguenot settlers in the seaboard colonies.

These Protestant French were not overjoyed at having their Catholic countrymen forced upon them. Nor were the French-speaking Acadians welcome in English-speaking households. Only Connecticut made any provision for them, accepting about four hundred, and even then only by breaking up families. Réné Le Blanc, a Grand Pré notary, landed in New York with only his wife and two youngest children. Eighteen other children were scattered throughout the colonies. And when smallpox broke out on one ship carrying refugees, Philadelphia, the City of Brotherly Love, permitted it to dock only after many Acadians had died untreated. Then the Quakers nursed a few, but most were brusquely ordered to move on.

Several thousand people landed in South Carolina, but fled when the state legislature ordered them imprisoned.

For fifteen years Acadians wandered from place to place, seeking either to return home or find a colony that would welcome them. About fifteen hundred managed to get to Quebec, only to find themselves once more in British hands when the city fell. By 1766 some nine hundred who had drifted to Boston decided to go home as a group, come what might. Now, little more than ragged gypsies, they shuffled out of Boston on foot.

Many died on the four-month trek back to Nova Scotia. The survivors found New England settlers ensconced on their former lands. Too weary to protest, they colonized a stretch of wild land on the west side of Nova Scotia that today is known as "the French coast."

Almost a century later, American poet Henry Wadsworth Longfellow, moved by their story, wrote the epic poem *Evangeline*. It described one true case of a young Acadian couple separated on the day of their wedding by forced exile, and unable to find each other again. As romanticized by Longfellow, Evangeline spends her life wandering in search of her fiancé, at last finding him dying in a public hospital where she works as a nurse.

Some cynical French scholars believe that Longfellow's sentimental poem, in turning Evangeline into an Acadian folk heroine, transformed the Acadians from French outcasts into a people who proudly preserved their own identity and traditions.

Several thousand Acadians driven out of America's southern colonies made their way to French settlements in Louisiana. Because of their influence, French remained one of the two official languages of Louisiana for over a century. Until 1915 state law required French to be taught in public schools and all legal notices to be printed in French as well as English. Louisiana today still has almost a million descendants of the Acadians, known by the nickname "Cajuns."

Another half million are scattered throughout North America, many of them still stubbornly loyal to their language, their religion, and their tragic tradition.

4

France and 1776

THE complete victory of the British army forced a glum King Louis XV to sign the Peace of Paris (1763) which eliminated France as a colonial power in North America. He was compelled to cede Canada and all French territory east of the Mississippi except New Orleans. Of all the vast area he had called New France, nothing remained but two barren little fishing islands south of Newfoundland, and the West Indies islands of Martinique, Guadeloupe and Haiti.

The end of the Franco-British struggle for the New World united the colonists under the British flag. It also taught the leaders of the colonies, who had often been at odds with each other, the value of co-operating for their mutual benefit. Some began to feel that with the threat of hostile French and Indians removed, they now had less need of British protection.

Twenty-year-old Louis XVI ascended the throne of France in 1774. A dull, apathetic monarch, he had little interest in the growing colonial unrest in America. He spent most of his time hunting and making locks as a hobby while the extravagance of the nobility and Queen Marie Antoinette plunged France into financial chaos. Nevertheless, it was to Louis XVI that the colonists of America were forced to turn for help.

To have any chance of freeing themselves from the powerful British, the Americans realized they would need an alliance with Britain's traditional enemy. So in November, 1775, Congress appointed a five-man committee, headed by Benjamin Franklin, to carry on a secret correspondence with "our friends" abroad. The committee brought French agent Archard de Bouvouloir to Congress a month later. He secretly encouraged American leaders to believe that if they revolted, the ships they sent to France would return with substantial aid.

Louis' Foreign Minister, Charles Vergennes, was eager to use a revolt as an instrument of revenge for France's humiliation in the Seven Years' War. Moreover, if Britain could be stripped of her North American holdings, she would be weakened as a world power, and her whole empire might begin to fall apart. Then France could retake the territories lost at the Peace of Paris.

Vergennes was encouraged in his scheming by French dramatist Pierre de Beaumarchais, a secret agent of King Louis. Beaumarchais' personal sympathies, as a satirist and liberal, were strongly pro-American. He urged Vergennes to help the colonists with money and arms. The threadbare American agitator, Thomas Paine, whose pamphlet *Common Sense* had powerfully influenced the colonists' determination

46

to break with England, was put on a secret French payroll.

King Louis, knowing that France was not strong enough to fight Britain, was fearful of giving open support to the Americans. And he knew that if London and the colonies ever reconciled their differences after a French commitment to America, France would be caught in an untenable position that would find her helpless under their combined attack.

Vergennes soothed the King's fears by preserving an official neutrality but giving secret aid to the colonists. He was supported by French industrialists who hoped for a more favorable trading position in an independent America. The French people themselves strongly sympathized with the colonists' grievances, which were not too unlike their own, and also hoped to see their British conquerors humbled.

Perhaps most crucial of all, however, was the support of the influential French intellectuals, who were developing their own anti-monarchial movement. Voltaire praised the American Quakers for their love and practice of peace. Other French intellectuals waxed lyrical over the democratic village systems of New England, and the idyllic agricultural society of the Southern colonies. Rousseau saw the American Indians as romantic figures whose life style pointed the way toward a natural, unspoiled Utopia for all mankind. Even the King's own Minister of Finance, A. Robert Jacques Turgot, declared in admiration, "The Americans are the hope of the world. They may become its models."

Munitions worth a million livres ($200,000) were secretly siphoned to the American revolutionists in May, 1776. This aid was delivered by a fleet of forty vessels operated by Roderique Hortalez and Company, a fictitious front for Beaumar-

47

DU
CONTRACT SOCIAL;
OU,
PRINCIPES
DU
DROIT POLITIQUE.

PAR J. J. ROUSSEAU,
CITOYEN DE GENEVE.

—— fœderis æquas
Dicamus leges.
Æneid. XI

A AMSTERDAM,
Chez MARC MICHEL REY.
MDCCLXII

The title page from Jean Jacques Rousseau's THE SOCIAL CONTRACT (1762), in which Rousseau argued that no laws are binding unless agreed upon by the people. Rousseau's book greatly affected French thought and was a major force behind the French Revolution approximately thirty years later.

FRENCH CULTURAL SERVICES

chais' operations that provided almost all the arms and clothing for Washington's army. Vergennes also persuaded King Charles III of Spain to send some aid to the colonists by pointing out that if the British crushed the revolt, they would soon try to force the Spanish out of North America as they had the French.

Beaumarchais slipped his cargoes past a British naval blockade by sending them to the tiny Dutch West Indian island of St. Eustatius, paying the Dutch to ship them to the colonies. As many as 3,000 shiploads a year reached St. Eustatius. (In 1780 the angered British finally declared war on the Netherlands and raided the island to pluck out this thorn in their side.)

The Americans were grateful for France's unofficial assistance, but had hoped for open French participation after July 4, 1776. In December, 1776, Congress sent its most adroit diplomat, Benjamin Franklin, as Commissioner to France to spread propaganda for the American cause. Franklin urged Vergennes to go all the way in committing the French to the Revolution, warning that the American plight was desperate. If the French failed to become allies, the colonists were likely to have no choice but to accept British offers of conciliation.

"If we abandon them, England will make a reconciliation," Vergennes warned Louis XVI in turn. "France should stretch out her hand to those States, and their independence should be her work."

Franklin was tremendously popular with the French people who cheered his appearance on the streets. They regarded him as a shrewd, sensible philosopher with the common touch, a man whose inventions to better mankind proclaimed him a humanitarian. They considered his simple dress proof of his refreshing lack of pretension, and they admired his tolerant viewpoint. No diplomat seemed to the French to combine more attractively the unique virtues of the American spirit with an appreciation of eighteenth century enlightenment in Europe. (It was Franklin's unique genius that he was able to make the French forget completely that almost from the founding of the colonies they and the Americans had been shooting at each other during seventy years of Franco-British wars.)

As for Franklin's feelings toward the French, he later wrote, "I have spent several years in the sweet society of a people whose conversation is instructive, whose manners are highly pleasing, and who above all the nations of the world, had in the greatest perfection the art of making themselves beloved by strangers."

Fellow emissaries like John Adams, Arthur Lee and Silas Deane were envious of Franklin's popularity, and by assailing his character, sought to have the Continental Congress recall him. "Franklin's whole life," Adams raged from Paris, "has been one continued insult to good manners and to decency, outrages to morality and decorum which would never have been forgiven in any other American!"

But Franklin's influence in France was too great to permit his detractors to unseat him. They continued to be ignored while Franklin was feted by French nobility, scientists and intellectuals from King Louis to Voltaire.

Adams, unlike the diplomatic Franklin, was too proud to admit the debt the United States already owed to French aid. Piqued by Vergennes' reluctance to agree to an open alliance,

In 1778, while in Paris to solicit French aid in the colonies'
struggle for independence, Benjamin Franklin was received at
the French court. The seated figures at the right are Louis XVI
and Marie Antoinette.

NEW YORK PUBLIC LIBRARY

he snapped that America could win the war without it.

"I think," Franklin wrote in rebuttal, "an expression of gratitude is not only our duty, but our interest. . . . Mr. Adams, on the other hand, seems to think a little apparent stoutness, and a greater air of independence and baldness, will procure us more ample assistance."

Vergennes was so annoyed by Adams' arrogance that he simply ignored him and negotiated with Franklin.

Adams' reactions to Paris foreshadowed the French policy he would follow as Washington's successor in the White House. While acknowledging the beauty of French art, architecture and music, he wrote home that these would be of little importance to the United States for at least two generations, because Americans would be too busy building a new nation. He was more interested in French trade.

In another letter to his wife he admitted being impressed by one aspect of French beauty: "To tell you the truth, I admire the ladies here. Don't be jealous. They are handsome and very well educated. Their accomplishments are exceedingly brilliant, and their knowledge of letters and arts exceeds that of the English ladies."

But he couldn't make up his mind whether he considered the French an admirable or immoral people: "There is every thing here that can inform the understanding or refine the taste, and indeed . . . purify the heart. Yet . . . there is every thing here, too, which can seduce, betray, deceive, deprave, corrupt and debauch it."

Adams' ambivalence about the French characterizes the feelings of a majority of his fellow Americans even to the present day.

Thanks largely to Franklin, popular enthusiasm for all-out aid to the Americans swept France. French journals ran enthusiastic articles praising the colonists. A typical political cartoon, captioned "The English Corrected Like a Child," portrayed Britain as a gross infant, buttocks bared, being broom-spanked by America as France and Spain look on with smiling approval.

Some French aristocrats eagerly volunteered to fight in the American army without pay. The Marquis de Lafayette, a twenty-year-old captain of dragoons, declared, "At the first news of this quarrel, my heart was enrolled in it." He secured a commission as Major General from Silas Deane, an American agent in the pay of King Louis XVI. When the outraged British ambassador to France complained to King Louis, however, Lafayette was forbidden to leave for America. He escaped in disguise in a boat which slipped past two British cruisers, and landed in South Carolina. He sped north to report to Washington at Valley Forge. Asked his opinion of the ragged American troops he saw there, Lafayette charmed Washington by replying modestly, *"Mon General,* I am here to learn, not to teach."

Washington was suspicious when the young French aristocrat requested to be sent to Canada to win it for the Americans as "the fourteenth colony." He suspected that Lafayette was really a secret French agent sent to win it back as New France. Taking no chances, Washington gave him command of a division but sent him south to Virginia instead. But the American Commander in Chief was soon able to report to Congress, "He is sensible, discreet in his manners, has made great proficiency in our language, and . . . possesses a large share of bravery and military ardour."

Lafayette, who bought uniforms and comforts for his troops out of his own pocket, was a highly popular commander. In every respect he was a symbol of French friendship and aid for the American Revolution.

Not all the French volunteers received so enthusiastic a welcome, however. Many were penniless and in debt; they had been discharged from the French Army and were eager for employment. One French officer who landed in Charleston to join Lafayette wrote home, "When we said we were French officers, led solely by the desire for glory, and to defend their liberty, we were pointed to in scorn by the populace, and treated as adventurers, even by Frenchmen, who were very numerous in Charleston."

A crucial turning point in Franco-American relations came with the defeat of British General John Burgoyne at the Battle of Saratoga, 1777. When he surrendered his army of 6,000 men—a fifth of the whole British force in America—the news stunned London. Prime Minister Frederick North quickly prepared a bill offering the Americans everything they demanded "short of open and avowed independence."

As soon as the news from Saratoga reached France, Franklin's good friend Beaumarchais, now the King's secretary, eagerly hastened to inform Louis XVI that an American victory now seemed probable. He also warned Vergennes that the British were offering concessions to Franklin, who might be tempted unless France acted swiftly.

Alarmed, Vergennes sent for Franklin and agreed to two Franco-American treaties of formal alliance. The first provided that the United States and France would grant each other a favored-nation status in trade. The second, the Treaty of Alliance of 1778, guaranteed American independence "forever"; renounced all French claims on Canada, freeing it for American annexation; assured French possession of the West Indian colonies; and agreed that neither ally would sign a separate peace with Britain. When a confidential letter from France brought Lafayette advance notice that the Alliance was about to be consummated, he rushed to embrace Washington with tears of joy, crying, "The King, my master, has acknowledged the independence of America, and will sign a treaty to help you establish it!"

Shortly after the Alliance was signed, Lord North sent the Carlisle Peace Commission to the colonies to offer them total self-government except for matters of war and foreign relations. Washington urged Congress to ignore the Commission. The British emissaries were informed coldly that the only negotiations with London that could be considered would be those that included the withdrawal of troops and recognition of American independence.

The angered Commission appealed to the American people, threatening total destruction of the colonies if they did not abandon their new allies and make peace with the British at once. But the people, heartened by France's entry into the war, rallied behind Congress.

The French dispatched 6,000 crack troops under Marshal Jean de Rochambeau to support "the soldiers of Dr. Franklin," as Voltaire called the American army. There were rumors that the French had made Washington a Marshal of France, giving him at least equal rank with Rochambeau, but in fact Washington never received any real or honorary commission from the French army.

Treaty of Alliance

The most Christian King and the
United States of North America.
to wit, New hampshire, Massachusetts Bay,
Rhodeisland, Connecticut, Newyork,
New Jersey, Pennsylvania, Delaware,
Maryland, Virginia, North Carolina,
South Carolina, and Georgia: having
this Day concluded a Treaty of amity,
and Commerce, for the reciprocal
advantages of their Subjects and Citizens
have thought it necessary to take into
consideration the means of Strengthening
those engagements and of rendring
them useful to the safety and tranquility
of the two parties, particularly in case
Great Britain in Resentment of that
connection and of the good correspon-
-dence which is the object of the Said
Treaty should break the Peace with
france, either by direct hostilities, or
by hindring her commerce, and
navigation, in a manner contrary to
the Rights of Nations and the Peace
Subsisting between the two Crowns:
and his Majesty and the Said united
States having resolved in that Case
to join their Councils and efforts against
the Enterprises of their common Enemy,
the respective Plenipotentiaries,
impower'd to concert the Clauses &
conditions proper to fulfil the said

Traité d'alliance
eventuelle et déffensive

Le Roi Très Chretien et les
Etats-unis de l'Amerique Septentri-
=onale, Savoir New-hampshire, la
Baye de Massachuset, Rhode-Island
Connecticut, Newyork, New-Jersey,
Pensylvanie, Delaware, Maryland,
Virginie, Caroline Septentrionale,
Caroline Meridionale et Georgie;
ayant conclu ce jourd'huy un Traité
d'amitié, de bonne intelligence et
de commerce, pour l'avantage
réciproque de leurs Sujets et
Citoyens, ils ont cru devoir prendre
en consideration les moyens de
renserrer leurs liaisons, et de les
rendre utiles à la Sureté et à la
tranquilité des deux Parties, notamment
dans le cas ou la Grande Bretagne,
en haine de ces mêmes liaisons
et de la bonne correspondance qui
forment l'objet du dit Traité, Se
porteroit à rompre la paix avec la
france, Soit en l'attaquant
hostilement, Soit en troublant Son
commerce et Sa navigation, d'une
maniere contraire au droit des gens
et à la paix Subsistante entre les
deux Couronnes; Et Sa Majesté

or sooner if possible.

In faith whereof the respective Plenipotentiaries, to wit on the part of the most Christian King Conrad Alexander Gerard royal Syndic of the City of Strasbourgh & Secretary of his Majestys Council of State and on the part of the United States Benjamin Franklin Deputy to the General Congress from the State of Pennsylvania and President of the Convention of the same state, Silas Deane heretofore Deputy from the State of Connecticut & Arthur Lee Counsellor at Law have signed the above Articles both in the French and English Languages declaring Nevertheless that the present Treaty was originally composed and concluded in the French Language, and they have hereunto affixed their Seals

Done at Paris, this Sixth Day of February one thousand seven hundred and seventy eight.

C. A. Gerard   B. Franklin

Six mois ou plutôt, si faire se peut.

En foi de quoi les Plenipotentiaires respectifs, savoir de la part du Roi très Chretien le Sr. Conrad, Alexandre Gérard Sindic royal de la ville de Strasbourg et Sécrétaire du Conseil d'État de Sa Majesté, et de la part des États unis le Sr. Benjamin Franklin Député au Congrès général de la part de l'État de Pensylvanie ses President de la Convention du meme État, Silas Deane (cy devant Député de l'État de Connecticut et Arthur Lée, Conseiller ès loix ont signé les articles ci dessus, tant en langue françoise qu'en langue Angloise; déclarant néanmoins que le present Traité a été originairement redigé et arrêté en langue françoise; et ils les sont munis du cachet de leurs armes.

Fait à Paris le sixieme jour du mois de Février mil sept cent soixante dix huit.

Silas Deane   Arthur Lee

The first of two formal alliances between France and the United States signed in 1778. This treaty granted each country a favored-nation status with the other in matters of trade.

FRENCH EMBASSY PRESS AND
INFORMATION DIVISION

By floating French bonds, Finance Minister Jacques Necker raised $8 million in aid to keep the Revolution from collapsing in bankruptcy. And full use of the French fleet not only substantially increased the flow of supplies to the colonies, but also hampered the British in supplying their own forces.

The French navy arrived off New York in July, 1778, and for the next five years fought dozens of major sea battles with the British in American waters. In 1779, John Paul Jones, recently promoted to Commodore, went to France, where Franklin and the French Admiralty fitted him out with a task force of six ships. When his flagship *Bonhomme Richard* was crippled in a sea duel with a British convoy led by the *H.M.S. Serapis*, the British commander demanded his surrender.

"We have just begun to fight!" Jones cried. He fought so ferociously that before his ship went down he was able to force the British commander to surrender instead. Transferring his men and flag aboard the *Serapis*, he sailed off triumphantly with his squadron in the captured sloop of war.

This victory by an American naval officer commanding French-supplied ships thrilled the colonists, who saw in Jones' unconquerable determination a symbol of their own defiance of British might. They needed every ounce of such inspiration because by January, 1781—despite French help—the American cause seemed lost. Their unpaid, ragged, poorly fed troops were deserting in droves.

Lafayette's superior, Count Jean de Rochambeau, begged France for more reinforcements and money. "These people are at the end of their resources," he wrote. The French response was generous—an immediate shipment of six million British pounds (in gold) to enable Washington to pay his troops, and the dispatch of a new fleet with French troops under Admiral Count Francois de Grasse. This aid was also now in France's own interest, since America's defeat meant her own as well.

The French navy's most notable contribution toward winning the war was provided by Admiral Comte d'Estaing. In March, 1781, his fleet of twenty combat ships escorting transports carrying 6,000 French troops, defeated a British fleet trying to supply the forces of Lord George Cornwallis at Yorktown, Virginia. Cornwallis, his 8,000-man force cut off, had no choice but to offer his sword to Rochambeau, who led 31,000 French and 9,000 Americans in the attacking force. With Gallic grace Rochambeau insisted that the honor of receiving the surrender be given instead to Washington as Commander in Chief of all the American forces.

The capture of Cornwallis and the fall of Yorktown sealed the fate of the British. When the news reached Lord North, the Prime Minister groaned, "Oh, God, it's all over!" Lafayette jubilantly informed the French government, "The play is over—the fifth act has come to an end."

Congress convened for a service of thanksgiving. But the war still had an agonizing year-and-a-half to go before the guns of both sides fell silent.

The last battle of the Revolution took place at Blue Licks, South Carolina, on August 27, 1782. Colonel John Laurens, the last American officer of distinction to be killed in the war, died fighting off an attack by British Loyalists and their Indian allies. He was a grandson of French Huguenots who had settled in Charleston. Washington, a close friend, had sent Laurens to King Louis XVI with the appeal that had brought the French fleet into action off Yorktown. Laurens had also helped to crush Cornwallis.

(Another French descendant who contributed importantly to the American Revolution was the son of Gascon Rivoire. When he made his famous midnight ride to warn Massachusetts colonists that the British were attacking, he was better known under his Anglicized name: Paul Revere. And Francis Marion, the famous "Swamp Fox" who led the British on a wild goose chase through the Carolina swamps, was a New England Yankee of French descent. Alexander Hamilton had a Huguenot grandfather, Gouverneur Morris a Huguenot mother.)

With American victory assured, colonial leaders began to disagree about strategy. Some, feeling they had taught the British Crown a lesson, were content to patch up a "family quarrel" on American terms, resuming the old relationship with Britain but this time as an equal partner. Others, anti-British and grateful to the French, insisted upon an American foreign policy oriented exclusively toward France. The latter group was obviously favored by Paris.

But when Cornwallis surrendered, Lord North's ministry fell in Parliament, and negotiations with the British seemed feasible. He had been replaced by the moderate Marquis de Rockingham, who had brought about the repeal of the Stamp Act in 1766, and who considered the King's American policy the height of obdurate folly. He urged an instant peace.

Franklin's fellow commissioners in Paris, John Jay and John Adams, were eager to respond. Franklin reminded them that their orders from Congress explicitly instructed them to "make the most candid confidential communications on all subjects to the ministers of our generous ally, the king of France; to undertake nothing in the negotiations for peace or truce without their knowledge or concurrence; and ultimately to govern yourself by their advice and opinion."

But Jay and Adams outvoted Franklin and entered secret negotiations with Rockingham's agents. A preliminary treaty of peace with England was signed on November 30, 1782. Its terms were incorporated in the official Treaty of Paris signed a year later by Adams, Jay and Franklin, along with representatives of Britain, France, Spain and Holland.

Although Vergennes expressed public indignation at this violation of the Franco-American Treaty of Alliance, he was secretly relieved. His separate treaty with the Spanish obligated him to keep fighting the British beside them until Gibraltar had fallen. But that fortress had proved impregnable. Now Vergennes could plead the Americans' "treachery" as an excuse for signing a general peace.

The American violation of the Franco-American Treaty left a sour taste in many Gallic mouths, and the French could scarcely be blamed if a certain cynical and suspicious note characterized subsequent Franco-American relations. The United States could not be depended upon to keep its word, except when it was to the American advantage.

Yet at the same time French intellectuals viewed the American victory as a triumph of liberty and reason over suppressive tradition and autocracy. They now sought to muster their own forces for a similar revolution against Louis XVI.

5

The Guillotine Divides America

THE French revolutionists had a staunch champion in Thomas Jefferson. Jefferson was perhaps only second to Franklin in the affections of the French. When a French nobleman visited him in Monticello in 1782, he praised him as "a tall, kind man, not yet forty, with a pleasing countenance, but whose intellect and learning are substitutes for every exterior grace; an American who, without having left his own country, is at once a musician, a draftsman, an astronomer, a geometer, a physicist, a jurist and a statesman."

Jefferson succeeded Franklin as Minister to France in 1784. "I do love this people with all my heart," he confessed as he wandered about the country incognito. Eating with peasants and sleeping under their thatched roofs, he was very much aware of the poverty that existed amidst aristocratic splendor.

France, he was convinced, was a monarchy in danger. He

wrote Lafayette that the American Revolution had "awakened the thinking part of this nation from the sleep of despotism in which they were sunk." Frenchmen secretly preparing to follow the American example were among Jefferson's closest friends.

Meanwhile he sought to strengthen Franco-American relations by helping French trade penetrate the American market. British goods were preferred by Americans, who were used to them. The French held a champagne party for leading citizens of Boston to persuade them to switch to French wines. The Bostonians toasted France until they were all gloriously drunk, but they continued buying British sherry and madeira, and the masses stayed loyal to rum.

Franco-American trade also languished because the French only needed American rice and tobacco, paid less than the British, and imposed a high protective tariff against other American products. The only real commercial advantage France won for her help in the Revolution was a market for her silks and millinery, popular among American women.

French officials, grumbling about American "ingratitude," noted that while the United States couldn't seem to find enough money to repay France's wartime loans, it had plenty to pay for British goods. In reprisal, French ports in the West Indies were closed to American ships.

Such trade rifts did not deter the Founding Fathers from importing and using French ideas, especially Montesquieu's political theories about the importance of moderation, and tolerance of dissent, in the American Constitution they wrote at Philadelphia in May, 1787. Soon afterward Franklin wrote to a friend in the French Academy of Sciences, "Our Consti-

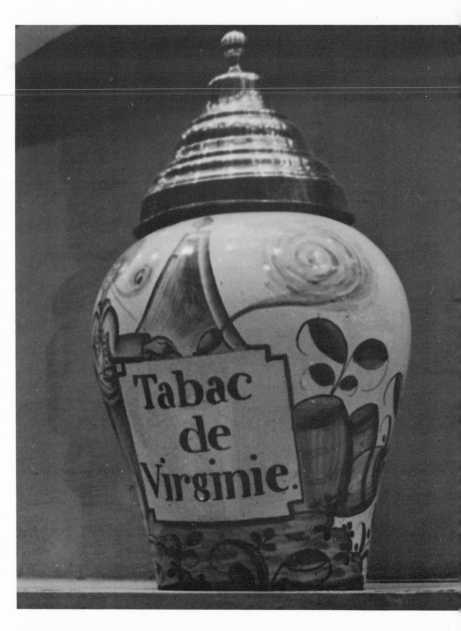

Tobacco was one of the most popular American commodities in France in the latter half of the eighteenth century.

FRENCH EMBASSY PRESS AND INFORMATION DIVISION

tution is in actual operation; everything appears to promise that it will last; but in this world nothing is certain but death and taxes."

French influence was also strongly manifest in the architecture of the new nation. Jefferson's blueprints for the capital of Richmond, Virginia, and the University of Virginia borrowed heavily from the French, and the plan that made Washington, D.C. one of the most beautiful cities in the world was drawn by French engineer Pierre Charles l'Enfant in 1791.

The French even helped name our currency—Jefferson and Gouverneur Morris named one coin a "dime" after the French term (pronounced "deem") meaning a tenth.

Many Frenchmen were equally enthusiastic about the new democratic principles of the Constitution in Amercia, and thousands sought to emigrate to the new republic. In 1786, the Paris office of the Scioto Company did a thriving business selling land in southeastern Ohio. French purchasers were lured by publication of letters from one over-enthusiastic French settler.

J. Hector St. John Crèvecoeur wrote, "If a poor, resourceless man with nothing but his hands to support him should ask me, 'Where can I go to settle down and live without care with no need of cattle or horses?' I would reply: 'Go to the banks of one of the streams that fall into the Ohio or the Scioto. All you'll have to do is to scratch the soil and put in your wheat, your potatoes, your cabbages, your turnips, your maize, your tobacco, and let Nature do the rest. All that while enjoy fishing and hunting.' "

Unwary Frenchmen who followed Crèvecoeur's advice soon learned the value of a little healthy skepticism.

One Frenchman who came to America in 1788 was Jacques Pierre Brissot, an agent of the French Society of Friends of the Blacks. The first abolitionist to appear in the United States, he startled Americans by his insistence that they had a moral obligation to free all their slaves.

A description of the stormy events that led up to the French Revolution was written by Jefferson himself. He was in the streets of Paris on July 11, 1789, just after Parisians learned that King Louis was preparing to use German troops to suppress their growing unrest. As his carriage crossed a bridge over the Seine, Jefferson saw an angry mob waiting for an approaching force of German cavalry.

"I passed through the lane they had formed, without interruption," he wrote. "But the moment after I had passed the people attacked the cavalry with stones. They charged, but the . . . showers of stones obliged the horse to retire and quit the field altogether, leaving one of their number on the ground. . . . This was the signal for universal insurrection, and this body of cavalry, to avoid being massacred, retired."

Jefferson had only contempt for King Louis and his extravagant Queen, Marie Antoinette. His sympathies were wholly with the revolutionists who stormed the Bastille in Paris three days after the street fighting he had witnessed. (Lafayette, incidentally, sent the key to the Bastille to Washington as a souvenir, and it was kept at Mt. Vernon.)

Jefferson's enemies, who called him a "French infidel," never failed to remind him that he had defended the French Revolution by insisting that "once in twenty years watering the tree of liberty with the blood of tyrants" was necessary. Yet

MEMOIRE
SUR LES NOIRS
DE L'AMÉRIQUE SEPTENTRIONALE

Lu à l'Assemblée de la Société des Amis des Noirs, le 9 Février 1789.

PAR J. P. BRISSOT DE WARVILLE,

Président de la Société des Amis des Noirs de Paris; Membre honoraire des Sociétés instituées pour l'abolition de la traite & de l'esclavage des Noirs à Philadelphie, à New-York, & à Londres, & l'un des Représentans de la Commune de Paris.

A PARIS.

Au Bureau du Patriote Français, rue Favart, N°. 5.

Chez { BAILLY, Libraire, rue Saint-Honoré, à la Barrière des Sergens.
DE SENNE, Libraire, au Palais-Royal.

20 Décembre 1789.

The title page from a 1789 dissertation on blacks by Jacques Pierre Brissot, president of the Paris chapter of the Society of Friends of the Blacks. Brissot toured the United States that same year, urging Americans to free all their slaves.

FRENCH EMBASSY PRESS AND INFORMATION DIVISION

This etching depicts the first singing of "La Marseillaise," the French national anthem, in 1792. The composer, Rouget de Lisle, is singing to a group of his friends.

NEW YORK PUBLIC LIBRARY

one month before the French Revolution broke out, he had proposed to leaders of the French Estates-General, composed of upper-middle-class reformers, that they work out a compromise between the people and the King in the form of a constitutional monarchy. They had sought to follow his advice, and he had played an advisory role in the French Constituent Assembly that abolished aristocratic titles and privileges, and adopted a French Declaration of the Rights of Man modeled after the American Bill of Rights.

And Tom Paine, who once had been on King Louis's secret payroll, did not hesitate to support the revolution against him. When England's Edmund Burke attacked it in his tract, *Reflections on the Revolution in France*, Paine, then in England, wrote a rebuttal called *The Rights of Man*.

"Monarchy would not have continued so many ages in the world," he charged, "had it not been for the abuses it protects. It is the master fraud, which shelters all others!" Men had the right to choose republicanism, Paine insisted, and not be forced to submit to titled aristocrats born to power. Why did Burke shed tears over the plight of an imprisoned Marie Antoinette or Louis XVI, but have none to spare for French victims of their despotism?

His British hosts were thoroughly outraged when he boldly hinted, "Never did so great an opportunity offer itself to England, and to all Europe, as is produced by the two revolutions of America and France."

Forced to flee from furious British mobs and police, Paine was given a hero's welcome by Republican France. The National Convention in Paris rose to its feet in a thunderous ovation when he entered the chamber. He was made an honorary

69

Built in 1369 to protect the palace of Charles V, the Bastille was destroyed during the French Revolution when, on July 14, 1789, a Paris mob stormed the fortress and freed the prisoners.

NEW YORK PUBLIC LIBRARY

citizen, along with Washington, Hamilton and Madison, and was elected as a revolutionary delegate to the new First Republic.

Paine aligned himself with the idealistic Girondists, many of whom were his and Jefferson's personal friends, rather than with their bloodthirsty rivals, the Jacobins. In January, 1793, he pleaded with the Convention to spare the life of Louis XVI because of the aid the monarch had given to the American Revolution. But a majority vote of 361 to 360 sent the deposed King to the guillotine.

The French National Assembly's decree proclaiming a "war of all peoples against all kings" sent shudders through Europe's other monarchs, but delighted most Americans. Their pro-French enthusiasm knew no bounds. Even the stolid Bostonians held a French-style civic feast of celebration on a street they re-named Liberty Square, where happy crowds devoured a roasted ox and two hogsheads of punch. The cry of the French Revolution, "Liberty, Equality, Fraternity," touched the American people, who *now* felt that they had more in common with the French than with any other people, despite differences in language, culture and tradition.

American naval hero John Paul Jones was living in Paris, having fallen in love with the city. He had been sent there to negotiate payment for the British vessels he had captured during the American Revolution and turned over to the French navy. Addressing the French Assembly on July 18, 1792, he declared that his affection for Republican France equalled his love of America. One week later he died and was buried in a French cemetary until later reinterment at Annapolis.

Not all leading Americans were delighted, however, by a

France turned republican. One month after the beginning of Washington's second term in office, the French First Republic declared war on Britain and Spain, and the Girondists asked the Americans to join as allies, citing the Franco-American military alliance. But the aristocratic Federalists—including Alexander Hamilton, Gouverneur Morris and John Adams— had no taste for fighting Britain once more, especially on behalf of a government whose bloody excesses against the French aristocracy revolted them. They were, besides, enjoying a highly profitable trade with Britain.

Washington carefully proclaimed American neutrality. Hamilton justified it by insisting that the Franco-American military alliance had been with Louis XVI, and had been ended by the guillotine. Furthermore, it had only been intended to provide American support for the French West Indies, not for any European adventures.

But at the heart of America's neutrality policy lay the basic fear of its conservative leaders that the French Revolution was a threat to world stability and order. They preferred to remain closer to Great Britain, a bulwark of the conservatism which, ironically, they had severely weakened by their own revolution. As a matter of fact, Thomas Jefferson and his followers were suspected of plotting a revolution against the Federalist Government to replace it with a French-style anarchy.

The Federalists, consequently, viewed with deep suspicion the growing number of French immigrating to the United States, although these immigrants did not necessarily constitute a threat to the newly established government. Some were landowners driven out of Hispaniola (Haiti and the Dominican Republic) by the revolts of native leaders Toussaint

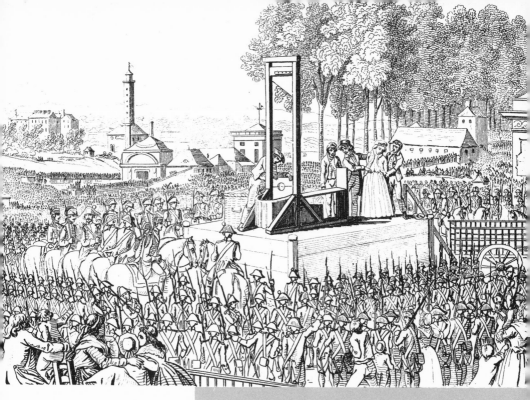

Marie Antoinette was
executed by guillotine
on October 16, 1793.
NEW YORK
PUBLIC LIBRARY

The official order for
the execution of Marie
Antoinette, scheduled
for 10 o'clock in the
morning at the Place
de la Révolution.

NEW YORK
PUBLIC LIBRARY

AU NOM DE LA RÉPUBLIQUE.

L'ACCUSATEUR PUBLIC, près le Tribunal criminel-révolutionnaire, établi à Paris par la loi du 10 mars 1793, exécution du jugement du Tribunal *de ce jourd'huy* requiert le citoyen commandant-général de la force armée parisienne, de prêter main-forte et mettre sur pied la force publique, nécessaire à l'exécution dudit jugement rendu contre *Marie antoinette Lorraine autriche Vve de Louis Capet* et qui les condamne à la peine de *Mort* laquelle exécution aura lieu *aujourd'huy a Dix* heures *du matin* sur la place publique de *La Révolution* de cette ville. Le citoyen commandant-général est requis d'envoyer ladite force publique, cour du Palais, ledit jour, à *huit* heures précises du *Matin*

FAIT à Paris, le *25 du 1er mois de* *179* l'an *second* de la République française, une et indivisible. *(vraie fille mercredy 16e: Cinq heure de matin)*

ACCUSATEUR PUBLIC.

4. Réquisition adressée par Fouquier-Tinville pour l'exécution de Marie-Antoinette l'Ouverture and Jean Dessalines. Others were ordinary Frenchmen migrating for land and a better life. Still others were French Canadians who settled in New England factory towns.

There was also an influx of French who had absolute Federalist approval—aristocratic refugees from the French Revolution and its extension into the French West Indies. Their cause was championed by Gouverneur Morris when he was appointed U.S. Minister to France in 1792. His open royalist sympathies outraged the Girondists, who were understandably irked at the Federalists' refusal to make America a co-belligerent in France's time of need. The least the United States owed them, they insisted, was an official neutrality that would work in France's favor by maintaining American supply lines with France's West Indies colonies. Hadn't the French helped the Americans secretly for two years before they did so openly?

In order to muster support, the First Republic sent a charming, unpredictable minister to the United States. Citizen Edmond Genêt was instructed to do all he could to obstruct British shipping and win the Americans as allies. Landing in Charleston in April, 1793, he received enthusiastic receptions all along his route north to Philadelphia.

Genêt wasted no time in carrying out his orders. Even before presenting his credentials to President Washington, he commissioned four privateers to begin attacking British vessels along the American coast. Learning about this, Washington received Genêt with chilly formality.

Soon afterward, Jefferson, as Washington's Secretary of State, had to give Genêt a letter from the President which denounced his actions, pointing out that they were an infringe-

This illustration from the cover of HISTORY OF THE FRENCH REVOLUTION by A. Thiers depicts the masses storming the Bastille as a proclamation of the basic rights of man.

NEW YORK PUBLIC LIBRARY

ment of the sovereignty of the United States. The privateers, he was told curtly, would have to leave American waters and would not be allowed to bring their booty to United States ports.

The adroit Genêt quickly apologized, promising Jefferson that Washington's demands would be respected. Instead he began traveling around the country setting up a network of clubs whose chief goal was to overthrow the American government. He distributed leaflets which showed the President being guillotined and advocated "The Death of G—— W——." Hundreds of Americans not yet disillusioned by the French Reign of Terror cheered his attacks on the Federalists. "Old man Washington can't forgive my success," he boasted in dispatches to Paris, where the fanatical Jacobins had by now wrested power from the moderate Girondists.

But Genêt made the fatal error of overestimating the value of public support, and underestimating the power of the Federalist government. When he let one of his privateer captains sail a captured British vessel into an American port to be armed, Washington angrily told him it could not leave port. Genêt defiantly ordered it to put to sea.

Even Jefferson now had to agree that Genêt had seriously overstepped his bounds. "Genêt makes my position terribly difficult," he commented privately. He voted with the Cabinet to demand Genêt's recall. Washington told Congress that Genêt had sought to involve the United States "in war abroad, and discord and anarchy at home."

Robespierre, now in power in France, obligingly made an appointment with the guillotine for the Girondist-appointed minister who had so mishandled Franco-American relations.

76

In return he asked Washington to recall pro-Royalist Gouverneur Morris, the U.S. minister to France, who was obnoxious to the French government.

Robespierre sent a new French Minister, Joseph Fauchet, to America in 1794, with orders for Genêt's arrest. The terrified diplomat now appealed to the President (whose assassination he recently had urged!) for political asylum. Washington was troubled by the thought of having Genêt's execution on his conscience, and refused to extradite him.

Allowed to remain in the United States, Citizen Genêt applied his charm in a different direction and won the hand of the daughter of Governor George Clinton of New York. He became a gentleman farmer on the Hudson, and compounded the irony by becoming an American citizen in 1804.

Still indignant at French interference in American affairs and appalled at the Reign of Terror, Washington sent John Jay to England to negotiate an Anglo-American treaty. When he replaced Morris as Minister to France with another outspoken critic of the Jacobins, C. C. Pinckney, the indignant Jacobins refused to accept his credentials.

The Federalists quickly pounced on this "insult" as a pretext for whipping up war sentiment against the French.

The rise of the Jacobins to power, meanwhile, had sharply altered the fortunes of one famous American friend of the French Revolution. Tom Paine was accused of collaborating with the Girondists, who began losing their heads in October, 1793, and he was seized, stripped of his honorary French citizenship and flung into prison. He wrote several appeals to Washington, who refused to come to his rescue.

The chief reason Washington did nothing was Paine's book,

This etching dramatizes the Reign of Terror, that period of the French Revolution during which the Jacobins conducted mass executions of their political opponents.

NEW YORK PUBLIC LIBRARY

The Age of Reason, a devastating attack on formal religion. Church-going Americans raised a great outcry against Paine's heretical theories. Once he had been a hero of the American Revolution; now no American was more unpopular. He languished in a French jail until James Monroe, as the new Minister to France, won his release in November, 1794. Broken in health at the age of fifty-seven, Paine spoke bitterly about the man he had served in 1776. "In the progress of events you beheld yourself a president in America and me a prisoner in France. You folded your arms, forgot your friend, and became silent." He called the President a hypocrite.

In 1802 he left France and returned to America at the courageous invitation of a new President and old friend. Thomas Jefferson continued to be loyal to France, shrugging off the Reign of Terror by observing, "You can't make an omelet without breaking eggs." He viewed Paris as the European capital of democratic liberalism, and London as the center of reactionary royalism. He agreed with the *New York Journal* which stated in July, 1793, "Americans, be just. Remember . . . who stood between you and the clanking chains of British ministerial despotism."

It had saddened Jefferson when Washington, whom he had respected for his honest neutrality, had been persuaded by Hamilton to tilt American foreign policy toward Britain. This change of the balance of power in Washington's Cabinet had provoked him to resign in December, 1793 in order to lead the Republican-Democrats, the opposition party.

The Federalists (who developed into today's Republicans) and the Republican-Democrats (today's Democrats) established America's two-party system. Previously, political opposition to the government in power had been viewed as a kind of treason, which explains why the Federalists considered Jefferson a virtual traitor.

In a sense, the two-party system owes its origins to the quarrel between those who feared and hated France, and those who admired her. The Federalists attracted New England clergy who worried about French "atheism" and its effect on American youth; New England merchants and ship-owners who looked to Britain, not France, for profitable trade; Northern capitalists who dreaded the spread of the Jacobin revolution; and aristocrats who feared that the French "rule of reason" would mislead Americans into anarchy and mob tyranny.

The Jeffersonians attracted liberals and intellectuals; Southern planters opposed to pro-British Northern capitalists; factory workers, fishermen and other members of the American proletariat who identified with the French Revolution; and anti-monarchists and anti-aristocrats of every description.

Americans stood at a crossroads. In one direction lay London, in the other, Paris. Which way would they go?

6
Jefferson, Napoleon and Louisiana

"EACH party will use foreign influence as it needs, to dominate," observed Count Constantin de Volney, a visiting French professor of history expelled as a spy in 1797, referring to the ties of the two American parties to England and France.

The split between Federalists and Jeffersonians was aggravated by French and British interference with American shipping. Each power sought to frighten the United States into respecting its own maritime superiority during the Napoleonic wars. The Jeffersonians found particularly outrageous the British practice of impressing American sailors from captured frigates into the Royal Navy.

They were even more incensed when John Jay concluded a treaty with England in March, 1795. Silent about this affront to American sovereignty, it granted trade concessions to Britain in the midst of their war with France. The Jay Treaty, Jefferson charged, was an "infamous act . . . a treaty of alliance between England and the Anglomen of this country against the . . . people of the United States." Furious mobs burned Jay in effigy. When Hamilton, speaking from the Treasury Building in New York, tried to make a speech defending the Jay Treaty, he was driven from the balcony by a hail of stones.

The indignant French considered the Jay Treaty another betrayal by America. A new French government which took power in 1795, the Directory, ordered its American envoys to create as much mischief as possible in order to disrupt Anglo-American co-operation.

"If the French suppose the people of America will oblige the government [by remaining] passive under any and all kinds of injuries from France . . . they mistake the temper of our people," growled the *New York Herald* in July, 1796. "If France should be the aggressor, France will find the Americans foes."

Soon afterward a British man-of-war captured a French ship carrying diplomatic dispatches from Joseph Fauchet, French Minister to the United States, to the French Directory. They revealed that Edmund Randolph, Jefferson's successor as Secretary of State, had offered to influence the Cabinet and Congress against the British for a French bribe.

"Thus, a few thousand dollars would have decided between war and peace," Fauchet wrote. "So the consciences of the so-called American patriots have their price!"

London promptly forwarded Fauchet's dispatch to the President. Thunderstruck, Washington confronted Randolph with it at a Cabinet meeting. Randolph denied Fauchet's allegation, but resigned immediately. When it was discovered that the sum of $49,000 was missing from his government accounts, it was assumed that Randolph had, in desperation, sought a bribe from Fauchet to cover the shortage. Randolph later published a retraction he obtained from Fauchet, but its validity remained in doubt.

The Genêt affair, the Randolph scandal, the persistent pressures from both Britain and France, and the polarization of American opinion, convinced the President that the United States could only survive through maintaining strict neutrality between quarreling European powers.

So in his Farewell Address on September 17, 1796—which he wrote with the aid of Hamilton and Madison—Washington told his fellow Americans, "The great rule of conduct for us in regard to foreign nations is, in extending our commercial relations to have as little *political* connection as possible. . . . It is our true policy to steer clear of permanent alliances with any portion of the foreign world . . . [but] we may safely trust to temporary alliances for extraordinary emergencies." And he added, "My first wish is to see this plague of mankind, war, banished from the earth."

When he relinquished the White House to John Adams, the French Directory, weakened by insurrection as well as war, was facing bankruptcy. Its promissory notes (*assignats*) fell to less than one percent of their value; the government desperately needed a large foreign loan to survive.

Charles Talleyrand, Prince de Bénévent, the lorgnette-carrying Foreign Minister, was a highly sophisticated dandy. A fellow diplomat described him as "lacking principles, assuredly, but wit, never." He was blandly convinced that the Americans owed it to France to bail her out of her financial troubles, since without France, there might not have been any United States.

Utterly corrupt, he expected the United States to follow the common European practice of paying him a "reward" for his diplomatic goodwill. This expectation baffled a commission appointed by Adams, consisting of Federalists Charles Pinckney and John Marshall, and Jeffersonian Elbridge Gerry, which was sent to France to obtain a treaty that would balance the pro-British Jay Treaty and quiet the furor of the Jeffersonians.

When the American commissioners arrived in Paris in October, they were puzzled by their inability to win an appointment with Talleyrand. The reason for this became evident when three of his agents called on them unofficially instead. The agents demanded not only a $10 million American loan to France, but also $240,000 as "compensation" to Talleyrand for some alleged "insults" by President Adams. Without such a deal, the agents made it clear, the French fleet would continue to attack American shipping carrying British trade.

Their proposal shocked the Americans. But the pro-French Gerry shrewdly pointed out to his colleagues that the American government was, after all, bribing the Barbary pirates not to prey on American vessels. True, Pinckney and Marshall were forced to admit, but was a civilized great power like France to be dealt with on the same low level as a barbaric Tripoli? Besides, they insisted, they had no authority to bribe corrupt French officials.

"No," Pinckney insisted. "No, no, not a sixpence!"

He and Marshall rushed home to report to Adams, who submitted an indignant report to Congress, referring to Talleyrand's agents as "X, Y and Z." The "XYZ affair," as it became known in 1798, stunned and infuriated the American

Charles Talleyrand retained his position as France's Foreign Minister throughout three very different governments—the Directory, Napoleon's Empire, and the restored Bourbon monarchy.

NEW YORK PUBLIC LIBRARY

people. The dismayed Republicans were acutely embarrassed by the unprincipled conduct of a French government they had been extolling as an ideal. Jefferson privately blamed the Jay Treaty for the whole mess but, as Vice President under Adams, considered it his "duty to be silent."

French Minister Adet in Washington abandoned all hope of improving Franco-American relations. "Mr. Jefferson is an American," he wrote Talleyrand gloomily, "and as such cannot be a sincere friend of ours, for Americans are the born enemies of all Europeans."

Belligerent Federalists demanded that the United States at once join Britain's war against France. "Britain is now the only barrier between us," Senator George Cabot warned Congress, "and the deathly embraces of universal irreligion, immorality and plunder!" And at a dinner honoring John Marshall in Philadelphia, South Carolina Congressman Robert Goodloe Harper proposed a toast that swiftly became famous as America's answer to France: *"Millions for defense, but not one cent for tribute!"*

Hamilton forced Congress into a swift expansion of the nation's armed forces and fortification of its harbors. Washington was recalled from Mt. Vernon as Commander in Chief. The Franco-American military alliance was renounced, and a newly-created Navy Department began building more frigates to attack French shipping in the West Indies.

A two-year undeclared naval war was fought with France between 1798 and 1800.* American frigates seized over eighty

---

* A Quaker named Logan made a trip to France at his own expense to patch it up. Incensed Federalists passed the Logan Act, banning any private citizen from meddling in foreign affairs.

armed French vessels in the West Indies, losing only one sea battle. This success owed much to the British navy, which was controlling the seas on the other side of the Atlantic, as well as bottling up Napoleon's army in Egypt.

Disgruntled Republicans were outraged by Hamilton's use of the naval clash with France as a pretext for building up a large American army and for setting up West Point. Their attacks on such "wasteful extravagance" were echoed by President Adams himself. "At present there is no more prospect of seeing a French army here," he dryly told his Secretary of War, James McHenry, "than there is in Heaven."

Because neither Adams nor Talleyrand really wanted war, both prudently sought to wind down the conflict. Adams assured Talleyrand that the United States sought only respect for commercial ships flying the Stars and Stripes. Talleyrand, in a new tone of reasonableness, informed Adams that France was lifting its embargo on the ships and ordering her fleet to consider them neutrals and leave them alone.

Talleyrand even assured Adams that France would now welcome any American minister to Paris—even Pinckney. As for the XYZ affair, Talleyrand explained urbanely, the blackmailers who had claimed to be representing him were imposters. In fact, the French Directory had even then been preparing for treaty negotiations with the commissioners, but the Americans had secluded themselves in a hotel, and then mysteriously rushed back to Washington. The Jeffersonians were quick to accept this dubious explanation, and branded the XYZ affair a Federalist hoax perpetrated by Hamilton war hawks. But anti-French sentiment was now at high tide in the United States.

Robespierre's Reign of Terror was brought to an end with his execution on July 27, 1794.

NEW YORK PUBLIC LIBRARY

Each change of regime in France during the 1790's had driven a new crop of French refugees into America. In a nation that still had only five million people—about half the present population of New York City alone—the votes of 25,000 French refugees were important. So the Federalists used the uproar over the XYZ affair as a pretext for depriving them of their votes, which were solidly pro-Jefferson.

The Federalists pushed the Alien and Sedition Acts of 1798 through Congress. Naturalization was made more difficult, and the President was empowered to deport any aliens, i.e., Frenchmen whose influence he considered dangerous to American security. Anyone speaking, writing or publishing criticism of the President or Congress was subject to fine and imprisonment.

Jefferson and Madison were outraged by the Alien and Sedition Acts, under which twenty-five editors and printers who supported the Republicans were arrested. They won passage of the Kentucky and Virginia Resolutions, state edicts that nullified the Sedition Acts on the grounds of unconstitutionality. But meanwhile over a dozen shiploads of Frenchmen had left the country to escape persecution by the Federalists.

Adams, who had had misgivings about the Acts, resisted when Hamilton tried to push him further into declaring war on France. Instead, he decided to send a new commission to France to work out a peaceful settlement of Franco-American differences. Hamilton became indignant and severed relations.

A coup d'etat in November, 1799, had replaced the French Directory with a Consulate government—Napoleon Bonaparte was First Consul. To consolidate his power in Europe, Napoleon needed peace with the United States. So he welcomed

Adams' new commission and agreed to a Franco-American treaty of commerce and maritime relations.

This Convention of 1800 also officially released the United States from the Franco-American military alliance of 1778 which the Federalists had refused to honor. In exchange, the United States agreed to settle claims against France for illegal seizure of American ships and cargoes during the early 1790's. Adams felt comfortable doing business with Napoleon because France was now no longer the violently radical republic that the aristocratic Federalists had feared. Considering his treaty with Napoleon his finest hour, Adams requested that it be included in his epitaph: "Here lies John Adams, who took upon himself the responsibility for peace with France in the year 1800."

Although he had achieved reconciliation, his split with Hamilton wrecked the Federalist Party. The Republicans won the elections of 1800. Thomas Jefferson, France's staunchest American defender, entered the White House.

Polarization over France, meanwhile, had become so extreme that Americans had even begun judging each other's political sympathies by what they ate. Taverns serving French or British foods attracted travelers of opposite views. Federalists were outraged when Jefferson took a French cook to the White House with him. Patrick Henry, indignant at the new President's acquired taste for French wines and cooking, was known to have criticized him for having "abjured his native victuals."

With Jefferson's election, the repressive Alien and Sedition Acts became dead letters, and the nation embarked on a new foreign policy. The new President was determined to re-

Napoleon Bonaparte became First Consul of France after the overthrow of the Directory in 1799.

NEW YORK PUBLIC LIBRARY

establish a warm relationship with the French, but soon found himself exasperated by his dealings with Napoleon.

The trouble was over Louisiana.

In November, 1762, France had transferred her Louisiana territory to Spain as part of an international settlement. Spanish law and language had officially replaced the French, but the colony remained essentially Gallic, especially with the arrival of the Acadian exiles from Nova Scotia. Intermarriage of the French and Spanish populations in New Orleans had created an attractive new generation called Creoles. The curious situation in Louisiana was reflected in $10 notes, issued by Spanish-speaking tellers in New Orleans banks, with one side printed in English, the other in French.

In October, 1800, Napoleon, seeking to revive France's colonial empire in North America, decided to reclaim Louisiana. Under the secret treaty of San Ildefonso, the Spanish agreed to give Louisiana back to Napoleon, in exchange for the French-held Duchy of Tuscany in Italy. A condition was attached: Napoleon must never cede Louisiana to either the United States or Britain, the two greatest threats to Spain's American colonies. (The cynical Napoleon, incidentally, kept neither part of his bargain.)

It was almost three years before he even bothered to take possession of the territory. Spain continued in temporary control of what was literally a no-man's-land, abandoned by one country, as yet unclaimed by another.

Louisiana now cultivated sugar cane and cotton, crops that had been introduced from the West Indies. But its chief importance in Napoleon's plans was as a food supply base for Haiti. The Haitians were more occupied with growing valuable cash crops of sugar, coffee, cacao, tobacco, cotton and indigo than with raising their own food. Prior to 1780, a thousand ships and 80,000 French sailors had been employed by France in the highly lucrative Haitian trade. With the outbreak of the French Revolution, Haiti had become a black republic demanding independence; Napoleon, however, was determined to hold on to it.

Jefferson was upset when he was apprised of Napoleon's secret treaty of San Ildefonso.

"The day that France takes New Orleans," he wrote his Minister to France, Robert Livingston, "we must marry ourselves to the British fleet and nation." Despite his fondness for the French, he now agreed with Washington's belief in "temporary alliances for extraordinary emergencies."

In October, 1802, the Spanish governor of Louisiana closed the port of New Orleans to all American boats on the Mississippi, much as Egypt later closed the Suez Canal to the ships of Israel. This action shocked and infuriated 50,000 American farmers in the valleys of the Ohio and Tennessee Rivers. Separated from Eastern markets and seaports by the Allegheny Mountains, they had always depended upon the Mississippi as their sole means of delivery. They urged Jefferson to seize New Orleans.

A French colonial official, Pierre de Laussat, landed there in March, 1803, to prepare for the arrival of a French army to take over Louisiana for Napoleon. News of his arrival increased the uproar. Having the Spanish in Louisiana controlling the Mississippi Valley had been irksome, but at least there had been no military threat to the United States. Having a war-minded France under Napoleon in America's back yard was another matter, especially since Spain was now rumored to be negotiating with Napoleon to turn the Floridas over to him as well.

"The cession of Louisiana and the Floridas by Spain to France," Jefferson declared, "works most sorely on the United States. . . . There is on the globe one single spot, the possessor of which is our natural and habitual enemy. It is New Orleans through which the produce of three-eighths of our territory must pass to market. France placing herself in that door assumes to us the attitude of defiance. The impetuosity of her temper, the energy and restlessness of her character, render it impossible that France and the U.S. can long continue friends when they meet in so irritable a position."

It was becoming painfully clear to him that the France of the French Republic was not the France of the Consulate. As President, Jefferson's attitude toward Napoleon grew steadily cooler. He finally decided that Napoleon must be compelled to sell New Orleans and Florida to the United States.

He instructed Minister Livingston to bring this sale about, and also persuaded his friend James Monroe to go to Paris as a special envoy. Monroe was to speed negotiations before Napoleon could send an army to take Haiti and threaten New Orleans. Jefferson hoped that Napoleon's need for money would induce him to agree to the sale.

Meanwhile, the President who had once called the Federalists "war-mongers" did a little sabre-rattling of his own. Knowing that his letter eventually would reach Napoleon, he wrote his influential French friend in Paris, Dupont de Nemours: "Our circumstances are so imperious as to admit of no delay as to our course. The use of the Mississippi is so indispensable that we cannot hesitate one moment to hazard our existence for its maintenance. . . . So it is peace alone which makes us desire it; and which ought to make the cession of it desirable to France."

Monroe left for Paris with secret instructions to offer $2 million for New Orleans and the Floridas, but pay up to $10 million for New Orleans *alone* if he had to. If Napoleon refused to sell, Monroe was to press for a guarantee that American boats could use the Mississippi freely. The alternative, Napoleon was to be warned, was America's "closer connection with Great Britain"—a bald hint at an Anglo-American military alliance aimed against France.

On April 11, 1803, while Monroe was still on the high seas, France broke off diplomatic relations with England. Napoleon was now girded for the conquest of Britain, then Europe, and finally the world. On that same day Talleyrand gave an audience to Livingston, who sought to persuade him to sell New Orleans for $2 million. Livingston was flabbergasted when the French Foreign Minister inquired, "What will you give for the *whole* of Louisiana?"

Stunned, Livingston gasped a guess of $4 million.

"Too low!" Talleyrand replied scornfully. "Reflect further, Monsieur Livingston, and return to see me tomorrow." It was obvious that he had to be speaking for Napoleon. But why the French dictator was interested in selling the whole valuable Louisiana territory was a mystery.

The American Minister was unaware that Napoleon had been forced to abandon his scheme for a colonial empire. A French force of 34,000 troops had failed to wrest Haiti away from former slave Toussaint l'Ouverture, the Republican leader whose guerrilla forces had fought with fanatical te-

Lucien and Joseph Bonaparte, Napoleon's brothers.

NEW YORK PUBLIC LIBRARY

nacity. Between Toussaint's guerrillas and yellow fever, 24,000 of Napoleon's forces had died in the effort, and 8,000 more were dying in overcrowded hospitals. Napoleon was forced to pour in reinforcements for the meager 2,000 troops left fit for duty, and was reported to have shouted furiously at his unsuccessful generals, "Damn sugar! Damn coffee! Damn colonies!"

He recognized now that Haiti was unconquerable, and he had lost interest in New Orleans and the Louisiana territory as supply bases for it. Furthermore, with war against Britain at hand, he knew that West Indies bases could never be held against the superlative Royal Navy. And, if he could not suppress the natives of a tiny island, what hope could he possibly have of holding Louisiana against the combined Atlantic armies of the British and the Americans?

"I renounce Louisiana!" he told his generals. "I shall sell that worthless place and use the money to conquer the British!" His new plan now concentrated on making Europe into a single continental nation, under him.

As he explained later in exile on St. Helena, "One counts in Europe more than thirty million Frenchmen, fifteen million Spanish, fifteen million Italians, thirty million Germans. I would have liked to make of each of these peoples one single and same national body." He added, "Perhaps it was becoming possible to dream for the great European family of a Congress as in America."

But even Napoleon's own family was appalled by his decision to sell Louisiana. His brothers Joseph and Lucien were particularly shocked by his arrogant intention to bypass the consent of the French Legislative Chamber. Lucien later wrote

97

a full account of their quarrel. Joseph had warned that their dictatorial brother planned to make the sale to raise funds for war with Britain. "You know," Joseph had sighed, "I'm beginning to believe that he likes war too much!"

The Bonaparte brothers, seeking to confront Napoleon at the Tuileries, found him in his bath. He silenced their protests, snapping, "Think what you wish about this, but both of you had better resign yourselves to this business as lost. It was conceived by me and negotiated by me, and will be ratified and put through by me *alone!* Is that clear?"

Joseph bitterly prophesied that Napoleon's arrogance would end in disaster for all of them. Napoleon angrily jumped to his feet in the tub, spluttering, "You are insolent! I ought to—!" He sat down again violently, splashing a large wave of perfumed water over his brothers. His valet, witnessing this quarrel, fainted away out of fear.

When Monroe arrived in France to join Livingston, the Marquis de Barbé-Marbois, Napoleon's Finance Minister, took over the negotiations. He refused to accept less than $11,250,000, and also demanded an extra $3,750,000 to settle claims by American merchants for vessels seized by the French during 1797–98.

Despite the $10 million ceiling Jefferson had imposed on their bargaining powers for New Orleans, Monroe and Livingston were fascinated by Napoleon's offer of the whole Louisiana territory for only $5 million more. His impatience to conclude the sale made them fear he would change his mind if they tried to sail home first to get approval.

So on April 30, 1803, their hearts in their mouths, the excited American diplomats agreed and signed the treaty.

"This is the noblest work of our whole lives," Livingston exclaimed. "From this day the United States take their place among the powers of the first rank!"

Jefferson was delighted, but quickly realized that with the Louisiana Purchase he had also bought a fight with his political enemies. Worse, the whole hasty business was so illegal that his position was completely vulnerable, and could even lead to his impeachment.

"His Majesty Loves the Americans, But——"

HISTORY would verify the Lousiana Purchase as the biggest real estate deal and best bargain in American history. But to many Federalists in 1803 it looked like an expensive white elephant with a defective legal title. It was still in the hands of Spain, not France. And Napoleon's right to it had depended upon his promise never to sell it to the United States. Besides, the French Constitution forbade the sale of national territory without the ratification of the French Legislature, which Napoleon had refused to consult.

Some Federalists even charged Jefferson with becoming a "fence" for Napoleon's "stolen goods for Spain." Furthermore, the boundaries of the territory were indefinite, so that no one could be sure just what the big package contained. The only boundaries mentioned were the Gulf of Mexico in the south and the Mississippi in the east. The Federalists also demanded to know what constitutional authority Jefferson had which would guarantee Louisiana's inhabitants the rights of American citizens, as well as eventual admission to the Union.

"The Constitution makes no provision for incorporating foreign nations into our Union," Jefferson was forced to admit. "In seizi.ig the fugitive occurrence which so much advances the good of our country I have done an act beyond the Constitution. The Legislature must now ratify and pay for it; and then throw themselves upon the country."

He added hopefully, "The country will support us."

This confession was highly embarrassing to Jefferson, who had once criticized Federalist administrations for usurping powers not expressly granted the government in the Constitution. To escape this dilemma, he wanted to ask Congress for a Constitutional amendment. But Monroe warned from Paris that Napoleon, impatient for his money, would not brook any delay and might declare the sale void.

So Jefferson rushed a bill ratifying the treaty to the Senate. He urged Attorney General John Breckinridge, "What Congress shall think it necessary to do should be done with as little debate as possible and that in secret. . . . The less that is said about the Constitutional difficulty the better. It is desirable and necessary to shut up the country for some time." Such illiberal views and irregular behavior from America's greatest liberal were darkly viewed by Senator John Quincy Adams, son of the second President: "Jefferson attained power by heading the attack on General Washington's administration under the banner of States rights. Elected President, the first thing he does is purchase Louisiana, an assumption of implied constitutional power greater than all the assumptions in the twelve years of Washington and my father put together."

Jefferson admitted that he had stretched his Presidential power "till it cracked," but pleaded the practical advantages of his illegal action. "Is it not better," he pointed out, "that the opposite bank of the Mississippi should be settled by our own brethren and children than by strangers of another family?"

On October 20, 1803, by a vote of twenty-four to seven, the Senate approved the treaty with France. The Spanish in New Orleans then officially turned the Louisiana Territory over to the French. Prefect Lausset relinquished his authority three weeks later to William C. C. Claiborne, first American territorial governor of Louisiana.

Many of the French in the territory were determined not to change their ways simply because they were now, without their consent, American citizens. They insisted that the territory continue to be governed under the Code Napoléon, the new French system of civil law set up by Lausset.

At a New Orleans ball in 1804 an angry quarrel broke out when Creoles dancing a French quadrille were interrupted by Americans who had ordered the band to change to an English quadrille. "If the women have a single drop of French blood in their veins," shouted one outraged Creole, "they will not dance!" A full-scale brawl was averted by the immediate departure of the Creole women with their partners.

But Jefferson's bargain with Napoleon had won for his country the very heart of the American continent, reaching from the Mississippi back to the Rocky Mountains, an area more than double the size of the nation itself in 1803. To explore and measure its vastness, he sent Lewis and Clarke on an expedition that, in turn, paved the way for the later American claim to the huge Oregon Territory in the Northwest.

His purchase also made America master of the Mississippi, including the all-important port of New Orleans. It prevented the British from winning Louisiana as spoils in the Napoleonic Wars. And it avoided war with France, while ending French influence forever on American soil.

A different form of Gallic influence persisted, however—French culture. Distinguished French artists, scientists, architects, thinkers and naturalists who visited the United States during the nineteenth century often made a deep impression upon their hosts. Two famous examples were sociologist Alexis de Tocqueville and conservationist John James Audubon, who roamed American forests studying and sketching birds, and who inspired the American Audubon Societies named after him.

One talented Frenchman and Revolutionary War veteran, Major Pierre Charles l'Enfant, was hired by President Washington in 1791, on Secretary of State Thomas Jefferson's recommendation, to plan a new capital for the nation. Three commissioners were appointed to supervise his plans. But he proved so temperamental and exasperating that after giving the city of Washington its shape, and choosing the location of the Capitol, the White House and the principal streets, he was fired.

Perhaps as a wry comment, when French traveler Perrin du Lac returned from a trip around the United States, he published a book in 1805 reporting, "The guiding principle of Americans seems to be never to do anything as we do."

The youngest brother of Napoleon, Jerome Bonaparte,

visited Baltimore in July, 1803, while the Louisiana treaty was being debated. Then a nineteen-year-old lieutenant in the French navy, he was received cordially at the White House by Jefferson and introduced into Baltimore society. Falling in love at first sight with pretty Elizabeth Patterson, a wealthy merchant's daughter, he married her over the angry objections of Napoleon.

An amusing view of Jerome's young bride, as well as of the influence of French fashions of the time, was glimpsed in the letter of a Washington socialite who wrote in 1805, "Having married a Parisian she assumed the mode of dress in which it is said the Ladies of Paris are clothed—if that may be called clothing which leaves half of the body naked & the shape of the rest perfectly visible—Several of the Gent who saw her say they could put all the cloaths she had on in their vest pocket."

Napoleon refused to allow Elizabeth to be brought to France, and compelled Jerome to let his marriage be annulled on grounds that he had been underage. An indignant Elizabeth sailed for Europe, but was not permitted to land in any country under Napoleon's control. In Portugal the French Consul General boarded her ship to inquire politely, and pointedly, what he could do for "*Miss* Patterson." Elizabeth flared, "Tell your master that *Madame Bonaparte* is ambitious and demands her rights as a member of the Imperial Family!"

But she never saw her husband again, even though she bore his son, young Jerome, and refused to accept the French annulment. "I was sacrificed to political considerations," she declared mournfully. Napoleon III finally recognized young Jerome as a legal cousin, passing a decree legalizing his right to the Bonaparte name. Jerome's descendants included a

*Jerome Bonaparte, Napoleon's youngest brother, married a
Baltimore socialite despite the angry opposition of Napoleon.*

NEW YORK PUBLIC LIBRARY

Secretary of the Navy under Theodore Roosevelt, Charles Joseph Bonaparte.

When Napoleonic France and Britain locked horns in a new war for world supremacy in 1803, the United States became the leading neutral sea carrier of foreign goods. Its maritime trade quadrupled in just two years. Napoleon observed that America was becoming a maritime rival for England "that sooner or later will lay low her pride."

The French and British sought to strangle each other with naval blockades and counter-blockades, and their warships frequently plundered American vessels carrying cargoes for the "wrong" power. In addition the British navy continued to abduct merchant seamen from American ships and force them to serve as British sailors.

Despite outraged American protests, there was some justification for this practice. Many British seamen were serving in the American merchant marine because the wages were higher. Those seamen with British accents were assumed to be deserters, and were taken off American ships unless they could show naturalization papers. When Jefferson protested to the French against their seizure of merchant vessels flying the American flag, Napoleon sneeringly referred to the flag as "only a piece of striped bunting." Napoleon then ordered the capture of any American ship that submitted to British search or touched a British port.

This harassment of United States shipping affected everyone living on the Atlantic seaboard who depended upon exports and imports—eighty percent of the population. Jefferson called France and Britain two "leviathans," churning the ocean and throwing up waves high enough to drench the Americans.

Resisting cries by some for war, he asked Congress for an Embargo Act forbidding all commerce with overseas nations. For fourteen months American ships rusted in port or plied the limited coastal trade, much to the disgust of ship-owners who preferred the risks of ocean commerce, and the anger of New England workers and industrialists idled by empty wharves and ships dozing at anchor.

Jefferson was flooded with angry letters from bankrupt and jobless Americans, one of whom wrote, "You Infernal Villain, How much longer are you going to keep this damned Embargo on to starve us poor people?"

To make matters worse, in April, 1808, Napoleon passed the Bayonne Decree under which he seized and sold some $10 million worth of American ships and cargoes that had been seized before the Embargo Act was passed. Tongue in cheek, the French Emperor blandly explained that he was merely helping the United States enforce the Act, since any American ships abroad in violation of it must "obviously" be British vessels with false papers. Exasperated, Jefferson denounced him as "a cold-blooded, calculating, unprincipled usurper, without a virtue." Napoleon shrugged; he had been called far worse.

Just before leaving the headaches of the White House to a new President, James Madison, in March, 1809, Jefferson admitted the futility of the Embargo Act by repealing it. Madison passed a substitute measure called the Non-Intercourse Act that permitted trade with all nations except France and Britain. And in 1810, he sought to play one nation against the other by offering to lift the ban on whichever one was ready to respect American ships at sea.

Napoleon at Arcole, a village in northern Italy where he de-feated the Austrians in 1796.

NEW YORK PUBLIC LIBRARY

Napoleon promptly ordered his Foreign Ministry to announce that since "His Majesty loves the Americans," he was repealing all French decrees against their shipping, and would henceforth confiscate no American vessels. Britain refused to follow suit, leaving Madison no recourse but to drop the embargo against the French and keep it against the British.

Napoleon, who had no intention of living up to his promise, blithely went on snatching every American ship he could lay his hands on. The angered British, meanwhile, blockaded New York and stepped up the impressment of United States seamen.

The War Hawks of the Senate finally won a declaration of war against Britain in the spring of 1812, by a vote of nineteen to thirteen, while an amendment to declare war on France was defeated by a vote of eighteen to fourteen.

"I am not prepared to deny that the orders of England are infractions of our rights," cried influential Boston minister William Ellery Channing, "but when I consider the atrocities and unprovoked decrees of France . . . I am unable to justify the war in which we are engaged. . . . We deem our alliance with France the worst of evils, threatening at once our morals, our liberty and our religion. . . . The character of that nation authorizes us to demand that we be kept from the pollution of her embrace!"

Many in the Senate agreed but were too realistic to pit the country against the two greatest powers on earth simultaneously. "I will concede . . . the injustice of France toward this country," said Henry Clay. "I wish to God that our ability was equal to our disposition to make her feel the sense we entertain of that injustice."

As it turned out, the United States was barely able to prevent a British victory. They succeeded only because the British had their hands full with Napoleon, who was pinning their major forces in Europe. American attempts to invade Canada —one of the secret territorial goals of the War Hawks who forced the war—were easily repelled. By the end of the war, the American navy was battered and had almost ceased to exist, despite some earlier victories on Lakes Erie and Champlain.

French privateers were operating freely in the Gulf of Mexico. Jean Lafitte, among the most famous of these pirates who came to New Orleans from France in 1806, soon had a thriving business in sea plunder. When the United States sent a naval expedition after him, he was able to prove that he had spurned a £30,000 British bribe to help capture New Orleans. His offer to fight on the American side in that battle was accepted, and afterward he won a pardon for his piracy.

The British victory over Napoleon in Europe freed their huge sea and land forces to deal with the Americans. Madison prudently and swiftly accepted a British offer to end their war. The inconclusive Treaty of Ghent was embarrassingly silent on the issues that had led America to declare war on Britain; nothing had really changed.

At the beginning of the Napoleonic Wars, American sympathies had been largely with the French. (Nine United States settlements were named Arcola and eight Marengo, after Napoleon's early victories.) But by 1815 when he fell, over a dozen American communities were celebrating his downfall by naming themselves "Waterloo." "'Tis done!" exulted Gouverneur Morris. "The long agony is over. The Bourbons are restored. . . . Europe, rejoice!"

Napoleon after his defeat by the Allies in 1814.

NEW YORK PUBLIC LIBRARY

Lord Castlereagh asked Henry Clay, who was in London, what America would do if Napoleon now sought asylum there. "We should soon make a good democrat of him," Clay replied. Napoleon preferred to cast himself on the mercy of his conquerors, but his brother Joseph fled to America, where he and his large family lived for twenty years.

One famous French general came to the United States at the specific invitation of Congress in 1824—the Marquis de Lafayette. Making a memorial tour of the country, he stirred a great surge of patriotic feeling and was overwhelmed by tremendous ovations wherever he went. In gratitude for his services, Congress voted him a gift of $200,000 and some land.

Lafayette, back in France by 1829, had led an insurrection to topple King Charles X and replace him with an American-style republic, with himself as President. Charles fled, but the coup failed in 1830 when influential French industrialists, bankers and journalists saved the monarchy by placing Louis Philippe, the head of the House of Orleans, on the throne.

When Lafayette had returned to France in 1825, he had brought back with him a large chest of earth from Bunker Hill in which to be buried. He kept this chest of earth from "the sacred land of liberty" in his house until his death in 1834. When he was buried in Paris, it was in the American soil that he had carried to France almost ten years earlier.

But, surprisingly, the new King of France was also an admirer of American democracy. After the French Revolution, Louis Philippe had spent three years traveling around the United States. He had been intrigued by the tactics used by American politicians to woo votes, and had decided that what French royalty required to make it popular was a leavening of demagoguery, American-style. As monarch, he erased the royal fleur-de-lis designs from his carriage, and imitated President Andrew Jackson by throwing open his palace to all Frenchmen who cared to shake hands with the head of their nation.

When Jackson demanded $23 million as a long overdue settlement of claims involving French seizures of American ships and cargoes during the Napoleonic Wars, Louis Philippe offered $10 million on the condition that the United States slash its tariff on French wines by a third. Jackson agreed and the Senate ratified the treaty, but then the French Legislature balked, refusing to appropriate the payment.

Furious, Jackson denounced France publicly and threatened to retaliate by seizing French property in the United States. The indignant French Foreign Minister accused him of barbaric, "Red Indian" diplomacy. Louis Philippe sent part of the French fleet to the Caribbean to perform some menacing maneuvers. Jackson promptly put the American navy on alert.

In 1834 the French legislature finally voted the money required by the treaty, but only on the condition that the American President apologize for his anti-French remarks. Jackson, a man of explosive temper, was almost ready to challenge Louis Philippe to a duel. Cooler heads prevailed upon him to disclaim any intention to "menace or insult" France. But he told Congress sharply, "The honor of my country shall never be stained by an apology from me for the statement of truth and the performance of duty."

England's Prime Minister, Lord Henry Palmerston, mediated the quarrel. He pointed out privately to the French Minister of Marine that if it came to war, France, whose main fleet was tied up in the Mediterranean, would find it difficult to prevent the now beefed-up American navy from swiftly capturing French Guadeloupe and Martinique in the West Indies.

France then professed itself satisfied with Jackson's "explanation," the money was paid, and the whole tempest was allowed to subside.

8

France Looks at America

IN January, 1835, midway through the second administration of Jackson, a book was published in Paris called *Democracy in America* by a young Frenchman, Count Alexis de Tocqueville. It was a book of observations about Americans and their country which he had made during a tour with his best friend, Gustave de Beaumont, from May, 1831, to February, 1832.

The book became a best-seller on the continent; it was eagerly read by Europeans who were curious about what America and the Americans were really like. In an English translation it fascinated Americans themselves with its candid, perceptive view of them. It is equally relevant for Americans today, as a random sampling of Tocqueville's most salient observations, like those included in this chapter, clearly reveal.

Tocqueville was a highly intelligent assistant magistrate, small, dignified, with dark thoughtful eyes, aristocratic features and black hair which he wore shoulder-length. He was only twenty-six years old when he made the trip. He and Beaumont were disillusioned with King Louis Philippe, but feared that his overthrow and the establishment of an American-style republic would impair the freedom, dignity and value of the individual in France.

To observe a major republic first-hand, they won a commission to study the American prison system for the French Chamber, which was planning an overhaul of the French criminal code. "I have long had the greatest desire to visit North America," Tocqueville wrote a friend. "I shall go see there what a great republic is like; my only fear is lest, during that time, they establish one in France."

(Although they viewed Lafayette—a cousin of Beaumont's —as a vain and dangerous demagogue, they solicited letters of introduction from him to prominent Americans.)

In New York City, one such person introduced them casually to Governor Enos Throop, "without any ceremony whatever," in the parlor of a boardinghouse where the Governor was staying. Being assured that anyone could meet New York State's chief executive this way at any time, Tocqueville marveled, "The greatest equality seems to reign, even among those who occupy very different positions in society."

Tocqueville found Throop "a fine fellow but undistinguished," and wondered why the people of New York had singled him out for the honor of being governor. He was told, "The men of great talent would not accept such employ; they prefer trade and business in which one makes more money." Tocqueville sighed, "There in two words you have the American character."

After a week in New York his first impression was that Americans were individually attractive, yet boastful, vulgar and materialistic, without any philosophy of government or culture. An appreciation of some aspects of American life came to the two young aristocrats only gradually.

"I especially admire two things here," Tocqueville noted by June. "The first is the extreme respect they have for the law; alone and without force it commands in an irresistible way. I think in truth that the principal reason is that they make it themselves and can change it. . . . The second thing I envy this people is the ease with which they do without government. Each man here regards himself as interested in public security. . . . Instead of counting on the police, he counts only on himself. . . . Public force is everywhere without ever showing itself. It's really an incredible thing."

Perhaps, he began to reflect, there were a *few* things in the American system that France might profitably copy—particularly if "worst came to worst" and popular government came to France. In contrast to Woodrow Wilson who later sought to make the world safe for democracy, Tocqueville wanted to make sure that democracy would be safe for the world.

The two young Frenhmen were charmed and delighted with the cordial reception they received wherever they went. "Our arrival in America has created a sensation," Beaumont wrote home to his mother. The French Minister in Washington told them why: "Your mission will flatter the natural pride of a young nation which sees travellers from the old societies of Europe coming to learn something from it."

Their contacts, at first, were largely limited to the affluent levels of American society. In Boston, Tocqueville attended

Alexis de Tocqueville wrote DEMOCRACY IN AMERICA,
a classic study of American democratic institutions published in
1835.

NEW YORK PUBLIC LIBRARY

three balls and noted that American society women dressed in French fashions: "The French mode dominates in the United States, and people are perfectly in touch with the least revolutions that it undergoes."

He was far more impressed with Bostonians than New Yorkers: "Almost all the women speak French well, and all the men whom we have seen up to now have been in Europe; their manners are distinguished, their conversation turns on intellectual matters, one feels oneself delivered from those commercial habits and that financial spirit that renders the society of New York so vulgar." Beaumont added, "They live very well in Boston. They have but a single fault . . . drinking too much."

Traveling through slave-free New England, Tocqueville was interested in the treatment of blacks there: "In Massachusetts the blacks have the rights of citizenship, they may vote in elections. But prejudice is so strong that it is impossible to receive their children in the schools."

In Philadelphia the young travelers were impressed by the immensity of the city. Tocqueville noted wryly that it was the only city in the world where it had occurred to people to distinguish their streets by numbers and not by names. "Only a people whose imagination is frozen," he wrote home in amusement, "could invent such a system." He added hastily, "But we must not speak ill of them, for they continue to treat us admirably."

He found Pennsylvania politics as petty as the French brand: "These are all excellent people, but political rivalries, and above all small-town rivalries, preoccupy them almost as much as if they were Frenchmen. . . . It's not necessary to travel two thousand leagues to see such things as that."

The young Frenchmen were greatly taken with the belles of Baltimore. "The women of this city have a great reputation, and truly they deserve it," Beaumont wrote enthusiastically. "I saw a quantity of very pretty ones. They dress well, are very attractive, and excessively coquettish, though I am persuaded that this coquetry is not very dangerous for them and that it's a path in which they well know how to stop."

Tocqueville was critical of Baltimore tycoons who used their riches to acquire the status of a moneyed aristocracy: "Money is the only social distinction, but look with what *hauteur* it ranks people. In France . . . it would have been considered an insolent pretension on the part of the wealthy to set themselves off from the rest." He neglected to point out that French titles were an equally dubious distinction.

Traveling through the midwest, he marveled at the prodigal "waste" of land. If Ohio were part of Europe, he observed, over ten million people would be crammed inside its boundaries—almost the number of Americans living in the whole United States in 1831.

The travelers were shocked by the indifference of most Americans to the wretched condition to which most Indians had been reduced by the white man. "The Indian races melt away in the presence of European civilization," Tocqueville wrote, "as the snow before the rays of the sun. . . . Every ten years, about, the Indian tribes which have been pushed back into the wilderness of the west perceive that they have not gained by recoiling, and that the white race advances even faster than they withdraw. . . . [so] they overrun the country, burn the houses, kill the cattle, lift a few scalps. . . .

"A regular army then marches to meet them; not only the American territory is reconquered but the whites, pushing the savages before them, destroying their villages and taking their cattle, push . . . a hundred leagues farther. . . . The Indians take up their march to the west, until they halt in some new solitudes where the axe of the white will not be long in making itself heard again."

On a river trip to New Orleans they met Sam Houston, who explained that Indians were slowing up "progress," so the government had decided to move them west of the Mississippi. But he assured the Frenchmen, "The United States have sworn, by the most solemn oaths, never to sell the lands contained within these limits, and never to allow the white race to work itself in by any means."

The French travelers found much to admire in the American frontier wife. "It's against the solitude of the forests that she has exchanged the charms of society and the joys of the home," Tocqueville observed. "It's on the bare ground of the wilderness that her nuptial couch was placed.

"To devote herself to austere duties, submit herself to privations which were unknown to her, embrace an existence for which she was not made, such was the occupation of the finest years of her life, such for her have been the delights of marriage. Want, suffering, and loneliness have affected her constitution but not bowed her courage."

He described how the pioneers lived: "The house inhabited by these emigrants has no interior partitions or attic. In the single apartment which it contains, the entire family comes in the evening to seek refuge: this dwelling forms of itself a small world. It's the ark of civilization lost in the midst of an ocean of leaves. It's a sort of oasis in the desert. A hundred feet beyond, the eternal forest stretches about its shade and the solitude begins again."

In the Tennessee hills one December night they sought shelter in a rough-hewn forest cabin. The settler invited them to warm up in front of a huge fireplace that had a whole tree burning in it. "Near the fire was seated the mistress of the lodge, with the tranquil and modest air that distinguishes American women, while four or five husky children rolled on the floor, as lightly clad as in the month of July."

Tocqueville added dryly, "Under the mantel of the chimney two or three squatting negroes still seemed to find that it was less warm there than in Africa."

Irritated by repeated Southern assurances that blacks belonged to an "inferior race," he reported his findings that when black children were admitted to some Northern schools they did well. He was also sharply critical of those Northern states that piously condemned slavery, while refusing to permit blacks to vote or use public accommodations.

"With us white and black blood will never mingle," a Philadelphian told him. "The two races abhor each other, and yet are obliged to live on the same soil. . . . The blacks will arm against it, and will be exterminated."

In Louisville, Kentucky, Tocqueville asked a prominent merchant named McIlvain whether slavery prevented the industrial development of Southern border states.

"When the blacks are placed young in a factory," McIlvain replied, "they are as apt as the whites to become good workmen. . . . If the South is not as industrial as the North it's not because the slaves are not able to serve in the factories. It's because slavery deprives the masters of the [energy] necessary to establish and direct them."

Tocqueville also found that many Southern whites were reluctant to work in factories because even the poorest farmers in states like Tennessee owned one or two blacks to work for them. Those with a dozen or more slaves needed only to ride and hunt to live comfortably.

The French visitors were granted an interview with sixty-two-year-old John Adams. The second President told them that he considered slavery a great evil because it contained "almost all the embarrassments of the present and the fears of the future." He saw the growing polarization of North and South as leading to terrible consequences.

Adams also told his visitors that the excesses of the French Revolution had frightened Americans into ultra-conservatism. But Tocqueville found that violence seemed far more an American than French trait, especially in the South.

"There is no one here who is not carrying arms under his coat," a young Alabamian told him. "In the smallest dispute, you pull out knife or pistol. This goes on all the time."

Fascinated, Tocqueville asked whether such assaults were not punished. Assailants were always tried, he was assured, but seldom convicted. His informant called attention to five deep knife wounds on his head. Had he lodged a complaint?

"My God, no! I tried to give back as good." The Alabamian added significantly, "Our education is very [limited]. There is no regular system of schools, a third of our population cannot read."

The two French visitors did not neglect the official purpose of their journey—a study of American prison systems. In

Syracuse, New York, Tocqueville asked Elam Lynds, founder of the penitentiary, how he justified whipping prisoners.

"I regard whipping as the most effective and at the same time the most humane punishment," Lynds replied, "for it never injures the health and forces the inmates to live an essentially healthy life. . . . I believe it impossible to govern a large prison without using the whip, whatever the opinion of those who have seen human nature only in books."

Investigating jails in Philadelphia, Tocqueville asked permission to talk privately to prisoners in their cells. He reached two conclusions from these interviews—that putting first offenders in jail for trivial violations with hardened criminals tended to educate youngsters for a life of crime; and that prisoners preferred work to idle isolation.

Despite minor regional and class differences, Tocqueville observed, Americans were remarkably uniform in their dress, speech, habits and pleasures. He attributed this similarity to the leveling influence of a public education that created a national spirit of equality, and to the spread of uniformity through the restlessness that kept Americans on the move.

In France, by contrast, "every one lives and dies on the soil which has seen him born." The French class system, as well as sharp differences between city and village, also kept millions of Frenchmen strangers to each other.

The French were wrong, Tocqueville reported, in their concept of rough wilderness cabins as the homes of American "peasants." "You enter this cabin which seems the asylum of all the miseries, but the owner wears the same clothes as you, he speaks the language of the cities. On his rude table are books and newspapers; he himself hastens to take you aside to learn just what is going on in old Europe and to ask you what has most struck you in his own country. He . . . will gravely inform you what remains to be done for the prosperity of France."

Meeting the former Secretary of the Treasury under Jefferson, Albert Gallatin, the young travelers learned from him another key difference between their two countries. "With you, labour is cheap and land is dear," he explained. "Here the cost of land is nothing and the labour of man beyond price. . . . I should not advise anyone to seek his fortune in our wildernesses unless he has at his disposition from 150 to 200 dollars. . . . The greatest expense is the clearing."

Tocqueville was impressed by the extent of political enlightenment he found in the country. "The Americans are hardly more virtuous than others," he decided, "but they are infinitely better educated. . . . The mass of those possessing an understanding of public affairs, a knowledge of laws and precedents, a feeling for the the best interests of the nation . . . is greater in America than any place else in the world."

He marveled at the American sense of equality: "In France, whatever people say, the prejudice of birth still exercises a very great power . . . an almost insurmountable barrier between individuals. . . . Those prejudices don't exist in America. . . . It does not in any way prevent the intermarriage of families (that's the great touchstone). . . . Even though two individuals never meet in the same salons, if they meet on the public square, one looks at the other without pride, and in return is regarded without envy. At bottom they feel themselves equal, and are."

Tocqueville wondered why some Americans were willing to

sacrifice the comforts of the Atlantic seaboard to open up the rugged Western wilderness. Historian Jared Sparks explained to him that under American law, the oldest son almost always inherited the whole property of a family. Consequently younger children often felt compelled to emigrate westward to seek fortunes of their own.

John Quincy Adams, the sixth President, invited the French travelers to dinner. Tocqueville asked him why Western settlers seemed to live by a much rougher social code than the more peaceful citizens of New England.

"New England was peopled by a race of very enlightened and profoundly religious men," explained Massachusetts-born Adams. "The West is being populated by all the adventurers to be found in the Union, people for the most part without principles or morality . . . driven out of the old States by misery or bad conduct or who know only the passion to get rich."

Beaumont, who seldom missed any opportunity to observe America's fair sex, was amazed at the way they were ignored by American men. "The two sexes come together only to eat," he noted aboard a Mississippi steamboat. "As the Americans are not chatterers, it's seldom that a man speaks a word to a woman, even when they both know each other."

The American male, Tocqueville also noted, had "little or no time to sacrifice to women and seems to esteem them only as mothers of children and housekeepers."

An enlightened conservationist, he deplored an American compulsion to destroy timberlands: "The country-dwelling Americans spend half their lives cutting trees, and their children learn already at an early age to use the axe against the trees, their enemies. There is therefore in America a general feeling of hatred against trees. The prettiest country houses sometimes lack shade on this account.

"They believe that the absence of woods is the sign of civilization; nothing seems uglier than a forest; on the contrary, they are charmed by a field of wheat. . . . How beautiful these forests must have been before the hand of man had dishonored them! Now they can be compared to a beautiful woman shorn of part of her hair."

At the same time he was impressed by the American tenacity in blazing trails, roads, canals, and railroads through the forests they destroyed. "In France there are large and very concentrated populations through which winds no road, he noted, "with the result that they are more separated from the rest of the nation than half the world formerly was."

He pointed out, "In the Michigan forests there is not a cabin so isolated, not a valley so wild, that it does not receive letters and newspapers at least once a week; we saw it ourselves. It was especially in such circumstances that I felt the difference between our social state and that of the Americans."

Comparing the abilities of Americans and Frenchmen, he considered his fellow countrymen superb craftsmen but "a brute in all the rest." The average American, on the other hand, seldom equaled the Frenchman's skill in any one craft, but could do a hundred other things better. Tocqueville credited the American emphasis on "useful education."

"There has never been under the sun a people as enlightened as the population of the north of the United States," he wrote admiringly. "Because of their education they are more strong, more skilful, more capable of governing themselves."

Despite their different European origins, he noted, they had achieved a remarkable feeling of national unity. "They have neither religion, nor morals, nor ideas in common," he wrote. "Up to the present it can't be said that the Americans have a national character, unless it's that of having none. . . . What then can be the only tie which unites the different parts of this vast body?"

He speculated that it might be their common agreement to let each man's talents develop in any direction he chose, without hindrance or limits. "This people is one of the happiest in the world," he mused, but added, "I see institutions here which would infallibly turn France upside down; others which suit us would obviously do harm in America."

As an example of the former, the right of assembly to protest was freely used by Americans without harm to the nation but, warned Tocqueville, transferred to France it would be abused to the point of revolution. He was also dubious about the value of universal suffrage for France, which he felt would result in the election of uneducated incompetents to public office, because of the animosity of the masses toward the upper classes.

This had happened in America, too, he noted: "All the enlightened classes are opposed to General Jackson . . . [but] he has the mass in his favor. . . . The dogma of the Republic is that the people is always right, just as The King Can Do No Wrong is the religion of monarchial states. It's a great question whether one is more false than the other."

The election of men like Jackson, Sam Houston and Davy Crockett showed "how far wrong the people can go . . . to be represented by people of their own kind." It was deplorable that a "David Crockett, who has no education, can read with difficulty, has no property, no fixed residence, but passes his life hunting," should be considered qualified to help make the nation's laws in Congress.

He did not blame able men for refusing to seek public office: "To win votes one has to descend to manoeuvres that disgust distinguished men. You have to haunt the taverns and dispute with the populace: that's what they call *Electioneering* in America."

Although he was finding more and more to criticize in America, Tocqueville found himself impatient with some of the absurdities expressed to him about America in letters he received from France. He wrote his family, "Don't believe half the unfavorable things . . . told you about this country. . . . I admit that the inhabitants of the country are not all the most agreeable company. A great number smoke, chew, spit in your beard. But they do not the less form a race of very remarkable men."

He approved of the strong anti-military spirit he found among Americans: "The notions and habits of the people of the United States are so opposed to compulsory recruiting that I do not think it can ever be sanctioned by the laws. . . . A large army in the midst of a democratic people will always be a source of great danger."

As their tour drew to a close in January, 1832, the travelers were invited to the White House to meet President Jackson, whom Beaumont dryly described as "not a man of genius." He was surprised by the fact that no guards protected the salon where the President greeted them, and by the total absence of pomp, ceremony or ornate furnishings.

"People in France have got an altogether false idea of the presidency," he observed, adding reflectively, "The power of the King of France would be nil if it were modelled after the power of the President."

A soirée in their honor was tendered in Washington by Louisiana-born Secretary of State Edward Livingston. They were gratified to discover that at gatherings of Washington's diplomatic corps, French was the preferred language.

Beaumont marveled, "You would believe yourself in a Parisian *salon*." The French Minister to Washington wrote Paris that Tocqueville and Beaumont were "being greeted here by every one with the same eagerness and enthusiasm that they have encountered wherever they have gone."

As they left for home, Tocqueville tried to sort out the torrent of powerful impressions he had derived from his odyssey through the United States. He had come expecting to find verification of his belief that democracy was an inferior form of government, but was returning instead impressed by many, although not all, of its institutions.

Neither Republicans nor Royalists in France, he was convinced, understood the machinery of an orderly democracy like the United States. They confused it with the anti-libertarian tyranny of the First French Republic. "We have had in France in the last forty years every form of anarchy and despotism," he insisted, "but never anything resembling a Republic."

He expected all democracies in the New World, eventually, to slip also into tyranny through the abuse of power by elected incompetents. "It's through this . . . evil that the American republics will perish," he predicted.

Nevertheless, he saw much in the American experiment

worth imitating, especially the separation of church and state, the loose federal system that allowed strong local self-government, the independent court system that served to protect minorities from oppression by majority legislation.

The answer for France, Tocqueville believed, might be a modified form of popular government with indirect elections guaranteed to bring the most brilliant minds into the national government. It would have broad but strictly defined powers. He recommended borrowing from America a bill of rights for citizens, emphasis on the individual, and the freedom of all men to pursue their own roads to fulfillment.

Tocqueville's findings fascinated his fellow Frenchmen. They were all the more impressed because he was at the same time highly critical of many American shortcomings—the mediocrity of political leadership; the tyranny of the majority over the minority in violation of the Bill of Rights; the atrocious system of slavery; the unjust treatment of Indians, the original owners of America; and the poor judgment shown by millions of Americans when they exercised their right to vote.

But he showed Frenchmen how their country could benefit from the American example in other respects. He recommended curbing the authority of the central government and encouraging each commune to behave like an American state by looking after its own interests, choosing its own officers, making and enforcing its own laws. He had not met a single American who had not regarded "provincial liberty as a great good."

Even if the majority in America often made mistakes, he also pointed out, at least their laws had popular support and did not have to be enforced by a King's troops. There were, besides, checks and balances by two legislative bodies, by the power of government and Presidential veto, and by the system of independent courts. No American Napoleon, Robespierre or King Charles X could seize power to subvert liberty.

Tocqueville's remarkable study of America in the 1830's strongly influenced the liberals of Europe. They became convinced that the era of royalty was coming to a close, and that some constitutional version of Tocqueville's recommendations would shape continental governments of the future.

The classic *De la Démocratie en Amérique* prepared the way for Karl Marx's Communist Manifesto and the popular revolutions that arose in Europe in 1848, ending the Metternich era of royalist repression. In the last hours of King Louis Philippe's regime, it was Tocqueville who warned the French Chamber of Deputies, "At this very hour we are sleeping on a volcano—I am profoundly convinced of it!"

The next day revolution flared once more in France, and the Second French Republic was born.

Tocqueville was important to Americans as well because he held up the first clear mirror in which they could study themselves and the new society they had built. His honest, astute observations filled Americans with pride in their accomplishments, but also with serious reflections about their shortcomings.

If Lafayette had helped to make the United States possible, Tocqueville had made it confident but self-critical. Perhaps his greatest contribution lay in making the Old World aware that the New World had discovered a better, if more complicated, way of life than monarchy.

9

Another Napoleon

THE failure of the French Revolution of 1848 to develop a more equal and just society led some disappointed French idealists to seek another solution. Charles Fourier hit upon an idea that, ironically, had its greatest impact not in France but in the United States. He wanted to re-organize society and make it closer to the more natural state extolled by Rousseau. Citizens would be divided into self-sufficient "phalanxes" of four hundred to five hundred families each, and they would live and work together in communes. Marriage, which Fourier condemned as "slavery for women," would give way to the unsanctified "law of passionate attraction." Each person would choose his own occupation and work only "reasonable hours under pleasant conditions."

"The labor is itself of the nature of a fête," Fourier explained. "Brightly colored tents afford shelter from the rays of the sun or from rain. . . . Tasteful kiosks are erected at convenient distances and are supplied with exquisite pastry and sparkling wine. The laborers go to the field and return again accompanied by the strains of music and the sweet singing of youthful choirs." Each worker was to be paid a minimum subsistence, and surplus profits would be divided $\frac{5}{12}$ths to labor, $\frac{4}{12}$ths to capital, $\frac{3}{12}$ths to talent.

Among the 3,700 French members attracted by Fourierism was young Louis Napoleon, future Emperor of France. But in 1832, a showcase attempt to set up a phalanx near Rambouillet failed. No other efforts succeeded. In the 1840's, nevertheless, Fourierism was enthusiastically introduced to the United States by reformer Albert Brisbane. During a period of economic depression, he persuaded the iconoclastic publisher-editor Horace Greeley that it offered a better way of life for unemployed Americans.

This early-day Communism made sense to Greeley because of its plan for joint ownership and cultivation of land. Phalanx members would presumably be able to provide their own food, shelter and clothing, which would free them from dependence on city jobs.

Equally interested in the French plan were Nathaniel Hawthorne, James Russell Lowell, Henry Thoreau and John Greenleaf Whittier. Their support encouraged the establishment of over thirty different Fourierist communities in America during the decade of the 1840's. But Ralph Waldo Emerson asked Greeley skeptically, "Is Fourierism really in the American tradition, Mr. Greeley? I have always advocated self-reliance and individualism."

"How self-reliant can you be on three dollars a week to support a whole family?" Greeley replied. "How individual can you be as a factory hand in a textile mill?"

A great debate over the workability of French Fourierism in America was staged in New York City between Greeley and Henry J. Raymond, his ex-disciple. The plan, Raymond asserted, was attractive in theory, absurd in practice, Communist in spirit. "The Christian religion," he thundered, "is the only power that can reform society."

Greeley defended Fourierism. He pointed out that it was a way of assuring workers the fruits of their own labors, as well as protecting them against unemployment. But the Utopian phalanxes proved to be disasters. Adults quarreled. Children ran wild. Intellectuals preferred to philosophize rather than work the stony soil. Only one phalanx survived longer than six years. By 1847 the movement was dead.

Greeley bitterly blamed "the conceited, the crochety, the selfish, the headstrong, the pugnacious, the unappreciated, the played-out, the idle, and the good-for-nothing generally; who, finding themselves utterly out of place in the world as it is, rashly conclude that they are exactly fitted for the world as it ought to be."

(It is interesting that the basic concept of Fourierism has been revived today, and is getting a second chance, in the growing number of youth communes.)

Greeley, incidentally, decided to take a leaf from Tocqueville's book and go to France to give his fellow Americans a look at it through Yankee eyes. After visiting the Paris Opera in 1851, he wrote, "Such a medley of drinking, praying, dancing, idol-worship and Delilahcraft I never before encountered!"

He was appalled by the artistic glorification of war in the

painting collection at Versailles. He reflected sadly that France and America had one serious fault in common: electing generals as Presidents. French farming seemed to him primitive, placing as it did the burden of the work on women. What outraged him most of all was the way the French fleeced American tourists. Was there any hope for a country that charged visitors for the water they needed to wash up for breakfast?

On a later visit to Paris he managed to get himself arrested and gleefully went off to jail in order to report to *New York Tribune* readers on the French prison system. Confined in a dank five-by-eight dungeon with crude furnishings, he was incredulous when, released by the American Minister after three days, he was billed a jail "rental" fee of four cents a night.

When Napoleon Bonaparte's nephew came to power as Emperor of France (1852–1870), French-American relations again took a distinctly chilly turn. Napoleon III had aspirations of reviving the old French dream of establishing an empire in North America. At the beginning of 1861, when it was clear that civil war was breaking out in the United States, he decided that Americans would be too busy killing each other to enforce the Monroe Doctrine.

Britain now had Canada. Why not Mexico for France?

Forty years earlier, in fact, a Mexican delegation had offered the crown of Mexico to his uncle Joseph, then exiled in New Jersey, if he would lead their fight for independence from Spain. But the brother of the fallen Napoleon had replied, "I have worn two crowns; I could not wear a third. . . . Every day I pass in this hospitable land proves more clearly to me the excellence of the Republican institutions of America. Follow the example of the United States."

Napoleon III had other ideas. Establishing a Catholic Mexican monarchy would not only win powerful Vatican support, but would also bring him an enormous increase in French trade and prosperity based on the exploitation of Mexico's rich gold, silver, copper and zinc mines. He also needed Mexico's cotton plantations because the Northern blockade of Southern ports had cut off France's supply of cotton, idling many textile plants in Normandy.

He found his pretext for invasion when Mexican President Benito Juarez was forced to suspend payments on Mexico's debts to France, Spain and England because of financial chaos left by five years of civil war. Napoleon persuaded Madrid and London to join him in sending armed forces to compel payment. He used Zouave battalions from the Berber regions of Algeria and Tunisia.

Their red tasseled caps, oriental pantaloons and blue field jackets outraged the Mexicans. It was bad enough for Napoleon to invade their country, but to use African instead of French troops seemed to them to add insult to injury. The English and Spanish were also taken aback when Napoleon insisted that Juarez must pay him the exorbitant sum of twelve million pesos. Then in May, 1862, when he landed 30,000 French reinforcements, they realized that his actual motive was provocation, not settlement.

Unwilling to serve as cat's paws for a French colonial scheme, the English and Spanish withdrew. Their defection led Napoleon's empress, Eugénie, to exult in Paris, "Here we are, thanks be to God, without allies!" She obviously felt that from this point on France's allies would be more of a hindrance than a help to Napoleon's plans.

In June of 1863 the French army defeated the forces of Mexican President Benito Juarez at Puebla, Mexico, in preparation for Napoleon III's establishment of a Catholic Mexican monarchy.

NEW YORK PUBLIC LIBRARY

The French army swiftly smashed Juarez's forces at Puebla, opening the way to Mexico City. Napoleon had already decided on a pawn to be crowned Emperor of Mexico—an unemployed Austrian aristocrat, Maximilian, young brother of the Hapsburg Emperor, Franz Joseph.

Meanwhile, Confederate President Jefferson Davis hinted to Napoleon that Texas could be ceded to France in return for recognition and open support of the Confederacy. The French Emperor sounded out England about a joint intervention to force mediation favoring the South. But in September, 1862, the Union victory at Antietam dampened any British enthusiasm for such open interference in America's family fight.

So Napoleon decided upon a more subtle ploy: he would help the South by weakening Northern support for the war. That would at least help drag out the conflict long enough to let him secure his grip on Mexico as a French colony.

He sent a secret emissary, Henri Mercier, to Washington to see Clement L. Vallandigham, an ex-Congressman from Illinois and now recognized as leader of the Copperheads (Northerners who sympathized with the South). Vallandigham, in turn, contacted Horace Greeley, whose influential *New York Tribune* had expressed troubled doubts about the wisdom of continuing the war. Greeley was asked to discuss a plan for peace with Mercier.

"What has France to do with our war?" Greeley asked in astonishment. "And why do they want to talk to *me?*"

"Napoleon III is willing to serve as impartial mediator in a peace conference between North and South," Vallandigham explained. "France feels that your support of the idea would assure its success." Flattered, Greeley complied.

140

After a meeting with Mercier, he promised *Tribune* support for the French peace plan. Mercier then made a public announcement of Napoleon's offer to the State Department. It came as no surprise either to Secretary of State William H. Seward or President Abraham Lincoln, who already knew of the scheme through United States intelligence agents. They were also well aware that it was a scheme to keep North and South quarreling while Napoleon annexed Mexico.

Greeley's involvement, however, shocked Seward.

"Greeley has gone too far!" he told Lincoln. "How *dare* he interfere as an individual in the conduct of the war, entering secret negotiations with the French as though he were the government!" He icily rejected the French proposal.

At Seward's demand, Congress adopted a resolution in March, 1863, forbidding any foreign intervention in the Civil War. Vallandigham whipped up a storm of Democratic protest against Lincoln's Republican Administration for demanding a total victory that would leave America "a smoldering graveyard of charred bodies." He was arrested for treason.

Pleased with his success in deepening the turmoil over the Civil War, Napoleon III used Seward's rejection of his "peace" plan as a pretext to build ships for the Confederacy at French shipyards in Nantes and Bordeaux.

At his signal, French General Forey marched on Mexico City. Juarez fled north to set up a guerrilla headquarters.

The Mexican Conservative Party, led by clerics, landlords and army officers who opposed the reforms of Juarez, welcomed the French army with a symphony of church bells and showers of magnolia blossoms. They were stunned later when Napoleon billed Mexico for the cost of his intervention, even charging for the flowers the Mexicans strewed before Forey's troops.

At the French Emperor's direction, a deputation of Mexican Conservatives left for Europe to "offer" the crown to Maximilian. Although his pretty bride Carlota had been described to Napoleon as "wild to be an empress," Maximilian proudly told the Mexicans, "A Hapsburg never usurps the throne." He demanded proof that the Mexican people really wanted him.

Exasperated but amused, Napoleon ordered a "plebescite" among the illiterate Mexican voters that represented, according to one wry British diplomat in Mexico City, a call for Maximilian by "two Indians and a donkey." Maximilian signed a treaty with Napoleon promising almost unlimited French access to Mexico's treasury in return for military protection of his regime.

He and Carlota arrived in Mexico in April, 1864. Enroute to the capital city he distributed notices proclaiming, "Mexicans, you have desired me. . . . I shall be before all else a Mexican, and place the interests of my people before all others."

A well-meaning man, Maximilian actually strove to live up to that promise. But most Mexicans saw him only as a foreign usurper kept in power by French bayonets. Juarez's guerrilla forces kept up persistent raids on the French occupation troops. Maximilian was compelled to agree to wholesale executions of Mexican "bandits," which united the country even more against him. His only support came from the rich Mexican Conservatives and clergy who attended his balls and receptions at a gorgeous palace he built at Chapultepec. But they, too, turned against him when he upheld most of the reforms Juarez

*Maximilian, young brother of Hapsburg Emperor Franz Jo-
seph, was made Emperor of Mexico by Napoleon III in 1864.*

NEW YORK PUBLIC LIBRARY

had introduced, including nationalization of Church property, which cost him Vatican support as well. He also angered Napoleon by refusing to turn over the mineral-rich Sonora province.

In the United States, Massachusetts Senator Charles Sumner denounced Napoleon III as "Trampler upon the Republic in France, Trampler upon the Republic in Mexico." Referring to France's support of the South, he cried, "It remains to be seen if the French Emperor can prevail as Trampler upon this Republic!" By a vote of 109 to 0 the House of Representatives refused to recognize Maximilian.

"It does not accord with the policy of the United States," the House resolved, "to acknowledge any monarchial Government erected on the ruins of any republican Government in America under the auspicies of an European power."

Seward, worried over Napoleon's reaction to this Congressional belligerency, sent William Dayton, the Minister to Paris, to the French Foreign Office. Dayton was asked frostily whether he brought peace or war. He delivered a placating message from Seward reminding Napoleon that Congress spoke only for itself, not for the Administration.

But the end of the Civil War sealed the fate of Maximilian and of Napoleon's hopes for a French-American empire. Upon Lincoln's assassination, Maximilian sent a note of condolence to Washington and asked the new President, Andrew Johnson, for a conference to work out differences between royalist Mexico and the United States. Johnson ignored it.

Instead, he sent General Phil Sheridan to the Rio Grande with 50,000 Northern troops, an unmistakable threat to drive the French out of Mexico. With the Civil War over, restless

Union and Confederate veterans buried the hatchet and joined an "American foreign legion" to aid Juarez. Napoleon uneasily sent word to Marshal Bazaine, Commander in Chief of the French forces in Mexico, to halt all military operations against Juarez too close to the American border.

But now Seward, his forces in place, accused Napoleon of placing "that Austrian fellow" on a Mexican throne in violation of the Monroe Doctrine.

"Since when," replied French deputy Jerome David indignantly, "has a 'doctrine' enunciated in a message to one nation, assumed the category of 'law' for foreign nations? The Monroe Doctrine happens to be a paragraph in a political speech, foisted upon Latin America without a 'by your leave.' . . . Simply because the government at Washington happens to be republican in form, it cannot be contended that monarchies have no place in the New World."

But Juarez's forces, now backed by large supplies of American arms, were already chopping up Marshal Bazaine's army with elusive guerrilla attacks. The baffled French marshal, trained only for classical uniformed warfare, was trying to sort out guerrillas from bandits and ordinary citizens. To add to Napoleon's woes, costs of the military occupation were soaring far beyond the revenue he had obtained by taking half of Mexico's customs receipts. To make matters even worse, French anti-clericals were demanding an end to the war against Juarez, while French clericals denounced support of Maximilian because of his similar anti-Church position. And France faced a dangerous new threat from Prussia.

So in February, 1866, Napoleon was almost relieved when Seward demanded that he name a date on which all French

When French forces withdrew from Mexico in 1867, Juarez captured Maximilian, pictured here as he is about to face the firing squad.

NEW YORK PUBLIC LIBRARY

troops would be withdrawn. He quickly agreed to end his ill-conceived adventure by recalling all forces within a year. Abandoned, Maximilian wanted to abdicate at once. But Carlotta persuaded him to wait until she went to France to confront Napoleon. When she arrived in Paris the French Emperor tried to avoid her, but she forced her way into his apartment at St. Cloud and upbraided him so furiously that he wept.

But his decision to abandon Mexico was irreversible. Rushing off to the Vatican, she forced her way into the Pope's presence to demand that he pressure Napoleon into honoring his commitment to her husband.

Reports came back to Maximilian that she had become so overwrought that she had lost her reason, and had been confined in a Belgian chateau. She remained there for sixty years. Whether Carlota was truly mad, or had simply been disposed of by the powers she had embarrassed, was a moot point. The news shocked Maximilian, who prepared to abdicate and rush to his unfortunate wife.

But as the French army withdrew in 1867, Juarez's forces closed in swiftly and he was captured. Juarez ordered him court-martialed as a warning to other potential usurpers. Appeals for mercy poured in from such noted liberals as France's Victor Hugo and Italy's Giuseppe Garibaldi, but failed to save him from a firing squad. "I die for a just cause," he declared calmly in his last moments, "the freedom and independence of Mexico. May my blood put an end to the misfortunes of my new country. Long live Mexico!"

French journalist Georges Clemenceau, later to lead France in World War I, blamed Carlota for the tragedy: "Was it not her ambition that incited the fool? I regret that she has lost her

147

reason and cannot realize that she killed her husband and that a people are avenging themselves."

For years afterward the execution of Maximilian was a popular subject for French artists who painted the scene over and over, in subtle attacks on Napoleon III as the real culprit. The Emperor's police prevented one such painting by the great French artist Édouard Manet from being hung.

The ill-starred French adventure in Mexico between 1861 and 1867 led to the fall of Napoleon III three years later. Unsupported at home, unable to win an ally abroad, he fell before the Prussian armies of Bismarck.

The Maximilian affair had been European royalty's first important challenge to the Monroe Doctrine, at a time when the United States was least able to resist. Seward's determined stand after the Civil War represented a victory for the Doctrine, reaffirming it as an American policy that Europe never seriously challenged again.

10
"Lafayette, We Are Here!"

DEFEATED Southerners were not unappreciative of France's attempt to aid them during the war. Several thousand, unwilling to live in a post bellum South under Northern rule, made their way to Paris and its suburbs. They included such notables as Confederate Secretary of War John Breckinridge and General P.G.T. Beauregard. Their days were spent calling on each other, driving through the Bois de Boulogne, attending the races and playing cards.

Some continued to scheme in France for Southern independence. They welcomed Jefferson Davis when, through Horace Greeley's efforts, he was released from prison, and they wanted to introduce him to Napoleon. Davis refused, correctly convinced that the French Emperor's professed sympathy with the Confederacy had been utterly insincere and opportunistic.

The Southerners coldly ignored an International Slavery

Conference that opened in Paris in 1867, attended by the fiery abolitionist, William Lloyd Garrison, among many others. They were enthusiastic, however, about the Paris Exposition of that same year that brought Americans to Paris by the thousands.

"It is impossible for an American to visit Paris without enjoyment and instruction," declared the brother of General William Sherman. "The people of Paris are always polite, especially to Americans. The debt of gratitude for the assistance of France in our War of the Revolution is never forgotten by a true American." He added, "If I was not an American, I would certainly be a Frenchman!"

But many of the Southern expatriates grew homesick. On Christmas Day, 1868, President Andrew Johnson proclaimed a general amnesty, dropping all charges against ex-Confederate officers. For two years afterward nearly every ship putting in to Southern ports brought expatriates home.

Pro-French feeling revived again with the passing of the last monarchy of France, and the coming to power of the Third Republic in 1870. Once more the idea of "la belle France" brought sentimental feelings to the hearts of Americans who still thought of her primarily as "our glorious ally" of the Revolution. A few dissenters viewed her with amused condescension, however.

"The French are the most wonderful creatures for talking wisely and acting foolishly that I ever saw," scoffed poet James Russell Lowell while living in Paris during 1872–3. He added arrogantly, "They are a different breed. . . . I watch these people as Mr. Darwin might his distant relations in a menagerie."

But the revival of French cultural influence in the United States was in full swing. French works of art began to flow out of Paris and into the homes of rich Americans. A new Philadelphia City Hall was designed by an American architect who planned it as "a rich example of the spirit of French art." The massive New York City post office was done in "French renaissance" style, and quickly became a model for county courthouses and other public buildings springing up all across the midwest.

As Americans planned a centennial to celebrate the hundredth anniversary of their Revolution, the people of France raised $400,000 in contributions for a gift to stand as a permanent monument to Franco-American friendship. French sculptor Frédéric August Bartholdi was commissioned to build the largest statue ever made. Calling it "Liberty Enlightening the World," he designed it to stand in New York Harbor.

It was made in sections and sent to New York on a French battleship. The American people raised funds to pay for the pedestal and erection of the colossus, which was hollow and made out of copper sheets riveted to an iron framework. It was unveiled on Bedloe's Island on October 28, 1886. From "Miss Liberty's" crown, visitors could view the shoreline that welcomed Europe's "huddled masses yearning to breathe free."

The Statue of Liberty soon became a world symbol of American democracy. Its sculptor designed, in addition, statues of Washington and Lafayette which stand on the Place des États-Unis in Paris; a Union Square statue commemorating "Lafayette Arriving in America" for New York City; and the Bartholdi Fountain for Washington's botanical gardens.

While the French and American people were enthusiastically clasping "hands across the sea" in the euphoria of the centennial, the American Government watched with some dismay as a French company, headed by Suez Canal builder Ferdinand de Lesseps, undertook the construction of a similar canal through Columbia. Unhappy at the prospect of having such a strategic waterway in Central America under foreign control, Washington was relieved when Lesseps' project foundered.

By the time forty percent of the digging had been completed, some 16,000 canal workers had died of yellow fever and malaria, and the company was rocked by a scandal involving the alleged inefficiency and corruption of French ministers. Bankruptcy forced abandonment of the project.

President Theodore Roosevelt offered $40 million to the French creditors for the company's franchise and assets, including tons of French machinery that had been left to rot in the jungle. Columbia, however, balked at transferring the franchise without an exorbitant new fee for itself. Roosevelt promptly organized a revolution that broke away the canal area as the "independent" Republic of Panama. Panama then obligingly sold the franchise to complete the canal to the United States for only $10 million.

Washington remained suspicious of French intentions in Latin America. A large area of Brazil had been claimed by France, although the French had never attempted to occupy it. In 1894 gold was found in the north. French soldiers were moved into the area, and in May, 1895, they clashed with Venezuelan troops over the ill-defined Brazilian border.

Venezuela broke off diplomatic relations with France, charging that the French Minister had insulted the government.

United States Secretary of State Thomas F. Bayard warned the French ambassador against letting French troops cross into Venezuela "should French interests or ambitions prompt their invasion." Then Washington mediated a settlement of the clash.

It was clear to France that the United States now saw itself as the policeman of Latin America, limiting just how far the French could go in their dealings with countries under the protection of the Monroe Doctrine. This American role was underscored when the French sent a naval squadron to Santo Domingo, where a French citizen had been murdered during a dispute with a customs official of the island.

The French demanded reparations for the murder, and repayment in full of a debt the customs houses owed France. But a group of New York bankers had already taken over the customs houses to ensure collection of their own loans. Washington sent a warship to Santo Domingo to "watch carefully" over developments. The French prudently agreed to settle this dispute, too, without risking a confrontation with Washington.

At the turn of the century, American foreign policy was shaped by big business interests which sought to exclude both French and British trade from the American back yard. At the same time it tried to compel both powers to open to United States trade their own "sphere of influence" monopolies in China.

With the Presidency of Theodore Roosevelt, a military expansionist who believed in a strong navy to "show the flag" around the world, France and other European powers found that they had to reckon with the United States as a new and aggressive world power.

In May, 1905, Roosevelt appointed his good friend, Charles Joseph Bonaparte, as his Secretary of War. Because Bonaparte was the grandson of the Jerome Bonaparte whose American marriage Napoleon had broken up, the President asked the French government if they had any objections. They had none. Newspapers described Bonaparte as "a French aristocrat in feeling and deportment," although he refused to be considered French.

President Theodore Roosevelt, despite his international belligerancy, was essentially pro-French. In 1906 he demonstrated it. France had been working out secret treaties with England, Italy and Spain under which those powers were accorded spheres of influence in North Africa, in exchange for their support of a French protectorate in Morocco. But Kaiser Wilhelm II had no intention of letting Germany be shut out of a fifth of Morocco's trade. Going to Tangier in March, 1905, he proclaimed German support of Moroccan independence.

War between France and Germany seemed inevitable. The Kaiser called for an international conference on the Moroccan question, and asked Roosevelt to win France's consent. The American President did so, arranging the Algeciras Conference in Spain in 1906, to which he sent observers.

Roosevelt quietly influenced the Conference in France's interests, admitting privately, "I want to keep on good terms with Germany . . . but my sympathies have . . . been with France." The President persuaded France to agree to Moroccan independence, but won German agreement to let France train the Moroccan police, which was all the French needed. Five years later, at a strategic moment, the French took over Morocco completely.

The United States Senate ratified the Algeciras Convention reluctantly, troubled by Roosevelt's meddling in foreign disputes. They added a cautious proviso that such ratification was not to be construed as a departure from America's traditional policy of non-involvement in purely European affairs.

Early in the century France played an important role in the development of American aviation. Wilbur and Orville Wright had demonstrated the possibilities of powered heavier-than-air flight in 1903 at Kitty Hawk, North Carolina. Yet its significance had been ignored by the American government.

The more perceptive French paid the Wright brothers to bring their flying machine to France and develop it there. So in 1908 they began improving their biplane at Le Mans. The Paris *Herald*, witnessing one flight, reported that the plane rose to over forty feet, "remaining aloft almost two minutes as it circled twice, took turns with ease at almost terrifying angles and alighted like a bird." Before the year was out, the Wrights had set three world records, doubling their altitude, flying over sixty miles, and remaining aloft for almost two hours.

A dozen years later, right after World War I had been partly won by the Wrights' fabulous flying machines, the grateful French erected a monument to them at Le Mans.

Meanwhile, new ties were being forged between France and the United States on a cultural level. Around the turn of the century a system of exchange professorships was worked out for better understanding between the two countries. Professor Henri Bergson, who lectured at Columbia, was one of many French intellectuals invited to this country, while the American philosopher William James called his election to the French Institute "the greatest honor to which I could have aspired."

Mark Twain, however, took a wry view of what French lecturers might be able to contribute to American culture: "Religion? No, not variegated enough for our climate. Morals? No, we cannot rob the poor to enrich ourselves."

But leading American writers of the day deplored such moralistic evaluations of the French and urged their fellow Americans to adopt a broader viewpoint. Archibald Gary Coolidge, in his 1910 book, *The United States As a World Power*, attacked American hypocrisy over France's inability to sustain a stable government, use of birth control and production of "immoral" novels. He urged Americans to a broader appreciation of French creative vitality.

In the same year Henry Van Dyke, writing in his book *Spirit of America*, declared that true friendship between France and America was impossible as long as the latter considered France simply the "home of the Yellow Novel and the Everlasting Dance," while they continued to regard the United States simply as the "country of the Sky-scraper and the Almighty Dollar."

Franco-American ties were strengthened dramatically during World War I. When the war broke out in 1914, neutralist feeling was strong in America. President Woodrow Wilson, despite a deep personal sympathy toward France and England, felt obligated to assure the worried American people that he had no intention of involving them in a European conflict.

"I am not justified in forcing my opinion upon the people of the United States," he declared in April, 1915, "bringing them into a war which they do not understand."

A verse in *Life* magazine summed up the feelings of most Americans:

Five hundred miles of Germans, five hundred miles of French,
And English, Scotch and Irish men, all fighting for a trench.
And when the trench is taken, and many thousands slain,
The losers, with more slaughter, retake the trench again.

One of the firmest opponents of American involvement in
the war was Secretary of State William Jennings Bryan, who
said early in 1915, "The ambitions of France alone prolong
the war." He added later, "I congratulate myself that 3,000
miles of ocean separate the United States from the blood-
drenched field of battle."

The neutrality of the United States was understandable to
the French, but they were baffled by the anti-war crusading in
Congress that labeled itself "Americanism." As one French
politician of the day asked, "Who in France has ever thought
to preach Frenchism?"

However, some Francophile Americans sought to arouse
fellow countrymen out of their neutralist apathy. Poet Alan
Seeger was one of hundreds of Americans who volunteered to
fight for France by joining the French foreign legion.

"They sought neither reward nor glory," he wrote of the
volunteers, "nor did they wish to be distinguished from their
comrades in blue whose days it was their pride to share until
death." He was killed in action in 1916, and the posthumous
publication of his poem, *I Have a Rendezvous with Death,*
deeply stirred millions of Americans.

An American Field Service, organized by Steve Galatti,
drove Model T ambulances on the French battlegrounds.
Galatti barnstormed the United States to raise funds at pro-
Allied rallies, often against heated opposition. Incorporated

into the French army, his all-American ambulance unit served with distinction on the battlefields.

Many well-known idealistic young Americans who bought their own uniforms and paid their own transportation to France drove the ambulances and served as medics at the same pay as the French *poilu* (soldier)—5¢ a day. British poet laureate John Masefield called them "the very flower of American youth." They included writers e.e. cummings, John Dos Passos, Ernest Hemingway, Louis Bromfield and Dashiell Hammett, all of whom stayed in Paris after the war. Edouard Genet, American descendant of the famous Citizen Genêt, helped form the Lafayette Escadrille, a squadron of volunteer fighter pilots flying with the French air force.

Despite America's official neutrality, a flood of voluntary aid began to arrive at French ports in such quantities that the small wharves and few freight cars could not transport it. Distribution was then undertaken by an American War Relief Clearing House that organized hundreds of volunteer aide groups for France.

The French people in territory overrun by the Germans were in desperate need of food. By the end of the first year of war, many were kept alive only by offal thrown away by German military kitchens and the few skimpy purchases allowed in German canteens. Humanitarian Herbert Hoover organized an American Committee for Relief, which was soon feeding two-and-a-half million starving French civilians. By March, 1918, the Committee had provided shelter for thousands of the homeless and opened a large dairy providing French children with milk. Women volunteers nursed the wounded, staffed battlefield canteens and dispensaries.

American sentiment for official intervention on the side of the Allies increased sharply in March, 1916, when a German U-boat, without warning, blew the bow off an unarmed French channel steamer, the *Sussex*, injuring several Americans aboard. Wilson warned the Kaiser that another such incident would cause the United States to sever relations with Germany. The Kaiser promised to desist, in what was called the "Sussex Pledge."

But by January, 1917, he felt close enough to victory to renounce this pledge. To starve Britain out of the war, he ordered unrestricted submarine warfare. In April a grim Wilson asked Congress to declare war on Germany to make the world "safe for democracy."

Ex-President Theodore Roosevelt eagerly asked permission to raise five volunteer divisions to take to France. When he was turned down by Wilson on the advice of Secretary of War Newton Baker, who considered Roosevelt an amateur eager to play soldier, he tried to pull strings through the French Joffre Commission which was preparing to consult with Wilson. But they, too, rejected his idea as a "flash in the pan" political gesture that would provide France with only a few token regiments for newspaper headlines. They wanted a serious, all-out American army commitment to France's defense. Roosevelt was understandably embittered by such French "ingratitude" for his help to them at the Algeciras Conference.

Baker selected Major General John Pershing to lead the American Expeditionary Force, telling him brusquely, "I will give you two orders, one to go to France, the other to come home." For the rest Pershing was free to make his own decisions in consultation with the French and British staffs.

When he arrived in France in May, 1917, Pershing was asked to make a speech at the tomb of Lafayette. Publicity-shy, he designated one of his staff officers, Colonel Charles E. Stanton, to speak for him. Stanton concluded his address by saluting the tomb and crying out, *"Lafayette, we are here!"*

It was sheer movie melodrama. But in those relatively unsophisticated days such a gesture and phrase stirred tremendous enthusiasm, arousing hopes that at last, after four bloody and fruitless years of war which found them on the edge of exhaustion and defeat, the French and British would now be saved by the American Expeditionary Force. (Because Pershing was present, and spoke briefly afterwards as a result of the clamor raised by Stanton's speech, he was forever afterward credited with the famous phrase.)

By October, 1917, Pershing had the American First Division ready to enter the trenches for the final phase of their training at the side of French veterans. They were warmly cheered by the battle-weary French, who pumped their hands, hugged them and, of course, kissed them on both cheeks.

The "doughboys" were soon ready to take over whole sectors from the French on their own, fighting off German raids, trench lice and the terrible mud that made life on the battlefields an endless misery. The seasoned Germans at first regarded these American military amateurs with contempt, but they soon changed their minds.

The Commander in Chief of the Allied Armies, French Marshal Ferdinand Foch, viewed them primarily as auxiliaries. "Send me American regiments to be incorporated in our brigades," he commanded the American War Department. But Wilson insisted that Americans must fight in their own divisions under Pershing, feeling that in no other way could they develop and maintain the necessary esprit de corps.

American officers taking their units to France were irritated when French staff officers insisted on drilling them in French military strategy. "Who do you think you're dealing with?" exploded one West Point general. "Moroccans?"

Time had made little change in Franco-American relations. The French were still our good friends and comrades-in-arms.

And as exasperating as ever.

11
Friends Fall Out

IN the next few chapters we examine the political relationship between the United States and France, especially of the behavior of both countries during the wars of this century. This can help us see and understand the French better, and provide insight which was woefully lacking in Americans during World Wars I and II.

Even the Germans' desperate submarine warfare in 1917 failed to stop two million American soldiers from crossing the Atlantic to occupy trenches on the Marne. Their impact at Château Thierry under daring commanders George S. Patton, Jr., who led the first tank brigade used in warfare, and Douglas MacArthur, head of the Rainbow Division, who was awarded the Croix de Guerre for personal courage by the French, was decisive.

MacArthur, whom Pershing accused of "fighting his own personal war," was wounded in the crucial Allied offensive at St. Mihiel, but refused to be hospitalized. He was also gassed and wounded in the last great battle of the war on the Meuse-Argonne front, but escaped from a field hospital to take a heavily fortified key hill in the Hindenburg Line which had resisted all Allied attacks. The French were astonished by the front-line general who scorned the safety and comfort of the rear echelon to risk his life beside his men in the misery, filth and danger of battle. MacArthur returned from France a legendary "soldier's soldier," wounded three times, decorated thirteen times, cited for extreme bravery in action seven times.

The war created strong ties of personal affection between the French people and "Yank" soldiers, as well as to the people back home. "American hearts beat in unison with French hearts," reported André Tardieu, who later became Premier of France. "Rural friendship had developed into a comradeship of arms. . . . Hearts that had shared the some trials needed no interpreters to understand one another."

The songs America sang during the war testified to this bond in blood—"Over There," "Goodby Broadway, Hello France," "Somewhere in France Is a Lily," and "Break the News to Mother." But as suggested by another song, "When Yankee Doodle Learns to Parlez Vous Français," doughboys found gaiety and romance with French girls a welcome relief from the grim reality of war. Songs like "Hinky-Dinky Par-lay-Voo," "Mademoiselle from Armentières," and "How You Gonna Keep 'Em Down on the Farm After They've Seen Paree?" reinforced Americans' conviction that French morals were far "naughtier" than their own. But many French-Amer-

American troops marching down the Rue de Rivoli in Paris in 1918.

FRENCH EMBASSY PRESS AND INFORMATION DIVISION

ican romances ended in marriage, and American veterans settled down in France.

The French were grateful not only for the troops America sent but for her humanitarian aid. The American Fund for French Wounded, which distributed millions of surgical dressings and tons of hospital equipment, organized a civilian section to follow the line of trenches as they moved closer to the German border. It also provided housing, clothing, food and medical care for French families in liberated territory.

The American Committee for Devastated France provided social services, health services, children's services, well-stocked libraries, agricultural courses in canning, farm hygiene, equipment to build Boy Scout troops and equipment to aid the French blind and handicapped.

The French marveled at the community spirit of the Americans that led them to volunteer for public service. In France, such services were usually left to the government, which generally neglected them. Even the nursing profession had been unknown in France before the twentieth century. Although rich in political and cultural traditions, France lacked America's social conscience.

Many French people viewed the demands made upon them by the two-million-man American army with mixed feelings. They bitterly resented the requisition of their horses, houses and furnishings, especially for the two-thirds of United States troops who did not see battle. These troops, bored by Quartermaster Corps drudgery, unhappy with life in unhygienic, poverty-stricken villages where they were frequently overcharged for everything, were embittered in turn by French "ingratitude." And after the Armistice, many doughboys who were sent to occupy Germany in clean, comfortable billets decided that they liked their former enemies better than their allies.

President Wilson felt deeply responsible for the American lives that had been lost on the battlefield. He was determined to attend the Versailles Conference personally to make sure that the ideals for which they had died would not be discarded at the peace settlement.

In December, 1918, a fleet of French warships at the port of Brest welcomed his ship, the *George Washington*, with a twenty-one-gun salute. The French navy piped him over the side, and the French army provided a glittering guard of honor as he rode through Brest along corridors of police and soldiers. French citizens enthusiastically draped the city with flags and bunting. They also swarmed into the streets to shower him with flowers and roared homage in a reception that staggered him.

Wilson's arrival in Paris provoked an even wilder uproar. French President Raymond Poincaré rode beside him as two million Parisians broke police lines trying to touch the American President's two-horse Victoria which drove down the Champs Elysées, passing under the Arc de Triomphe now emblazoned with gold letters: HAIL TO WILSON THE JUST!

"No one has ever heard such cheers," commented journalist William Bolitho. "I, who heard them in the streets of Paris, can never forget them in my life."

Poincaré shouted in Wilson's ear, "I do not think there has been anything like it in the history of the world. You are very much loved, *M. le Président!*"

Overcome by emotion, Wilson bared his head to the French

Frenchmen crowd around posters announcing the conscription of horses and mules during the French mobilization of World War I.

FRENCH EMBASSY PRESS AND INFORMATION DIVISION

people and bowed in gratitude. The French government installed him and his wife Edith in the Palace of Prince Murat, one of the most magnificent estates in Paris.

Urged to visit the battlefields and devastated regions of France, Wilson refused, explaining that his uncontrollable Scots-Irish temper, inflamed by seeing what the Germans had done, would make it difficult for him to work for a just peace. The French were puzzled. A just peace was exactly what they did *not* want. Hadn't the Germans started the war? Hadn't they lost it?

Negotiating for France at Versailles was Premier Georges Clemenceau, who, as a correspondent in America years earlier, had applauded the impeachment of President Andrew Johnson for making a soft peace with the defeated South. He was now a wrinkled old man of seventy-eight with a walrus mustache and bushy white eyebrows.

The Peace Conference soon developed into a duel between him and Wilson. Clemenceau was incredulous when the American President sought to base the peace on the idealistic Fourteen Points he had articulated during the war. The Premier called Wilson "a dreaming schoolmaster," and scoffed, "*Le Bon Dieu* gave us Ten Commandments and we broke them. Now Wilson gives us his Fourteen Points. *Tiens* . . . we shall see!"

Determined to cripple Germany so that it could never again trample his country as it had done twice during his lifetime, he demanded that America join the British in guaranteeing French security. He also insisted that Wilson accept secret agreements he and Britain's Prime Minister, Lloyd George, had already made over the spoils of war.

168

Wilson replied by talking about ideals. But to Clemenceau ideals were a luxury France could not afford.

"Lloyd George thinks he is Napoleon," he observed at one point, "but President Wilson believes himself to be Jesus Christ!"

Wilson tried to soothe him by proposing that he be Conference President, "as a special tribute to the sufferings and sacrifices of France." Yet Clemenceau still refused to accept the American argument that a hard peace would only humiliate the Germans, and could have disastrous results. He insisted that all of Germany's colonies be divided up among the victors.

"Have you attempted to ascertain," Wilson asked, "whether your spheres of influence are agreeable to the people living there?"

Clemenceau glared at him. "What has *that* to do with it?" he asked.

Wilson was willing to go along with that part of the treaty if his allies agreed to set up a League of Nations to keep world peace. But Clemenceau cynically doubted that the American people were ready to obey edicts of an international authority. Only a weak Germany could guarantee the peace, he insisted, and only France knew how to handle the German problem.

"Pray, Monsieur Clemenceau," Wilson snapped in exasperation, "have you ever *been* to Germany?"

"No, monsieur," the Premier lashed back icily, "but twice in my lifetime Germans have been to France!"

"Your harsh terms may bring them back a *third* time!"

Clemenceau accused him of pro-German sympathies. Wilson's anger exploded and he sprang to his feet.

Here in the magnificent Hall of Mirrors of the Trianon Palace at Versailles, in June, 1919, the Versailles Treaty was signed.

FRENCH EMBASSY PRESS AND INFORMATION DIVISION

"No man in this room," he cried, "detests Germany, German militarism, German methods of education, more than *I* do. But if you destroy Germany economically, how can you expect her to pay the huge reparations that—"

Clemenceau rose. Wilson whirled upon him furiously.

"You sit *down!*" he roared like a schoolmaster to an impertinent pupil. "*I* did not interrupt *you* when you were speaking!" The astonished Premier slumped back meekly.

Wilson made an impassioned speech about the need to save the next generation from growing up only to be slaughtered in another bloodbath. His appeal stirred all at the Conference. Even Clemenceau gripped Wilson's hand.

"M. le Président," he rasped, "I want to say that you are not only a great man but a good one. *I am with you!*"

Only when the making of the peace was finished did Wilson risk the emotional strain of visiting the theater of war, the cemetery of the American dead at Suresnes, and the French hospitals where doughboys lay wounded.

The Versailles Treaty was signed in the Great Hall of Mirrors of the Trianon Palace in June, 1919, as the huge guns guarding Paris began to thunder. Their salute was echoed throughout France, in warships standing offshore, then in nations around the world. The war was over.

When Wilson came home, the Senate accused him of having been outwitted by Clemenceau and Lloyd George. They believed that he had let them carve up the world between them, and had then guaranteed their spoils by establishing a League of Nations that would involve the United States in "foreign entanglements."

At the same time, the French were angry at Clemenceau for

having failed to protect them by putting Germany in chains for a thousand years, so that never again would France have to fear a Teutonic war machine. They were scornful of American charges that Clemenceau had deceived Wilson at Versailles; it was Wilson, they said, who had forced Clemenceau to agree to a soft peace for Germany at their expense.

The angry French Parliament dismissed the Tiger of France, an act which many American newspapers saw as a repudiation of French-American ties. In the Presidential election of 1920 the American people also rejected their war leader's commitment at Versailles. No longer united by the threat of the Kaiser's Germany, each nation, pursuing its own self-interest, viewed the other with increasing disenchantment. Americans became convinced that the United States had been "played for a sucker" into pulling chestnuts out of the fire for France and Britain, and turned isolationist once more. The French, indignant at the American repudiation of Versailles, signed a separate peace treaty.

Wilson's Secretary of the Treasury, Carter Glass, had promised, "We will help France to rebuild; our industry will aid reconstruction." When Harding offered to redeem that promise, the French accepted the aid but privately grumbled that its real purpose was to keep American factories and workers busy instead of putting French industry back on its feet.

The peevishness that now characterized relations between the former allies was intensified in the summer of 1921 when France went to the aid of Turkey in a clash with Greece. The American press denounced France as "protector of the Crescent against the Cross, allying herself with barbarians against civilization." Newsreel scenes of French ships arriving in Turkish harbors brought hisses in American movie theaters.

Franco-American friendship chilled further during the Twenties when a few small European nations began paying their war debts to the United States, but France, England and Italy did not. Postwar inflation hurt the American taxpayer and made him doubly resentful of paying high prices and taxes he was told resulted from a default in repayment of over $10 billion in wartime and postwar loans to the Allies.

The Allies proposed a smaller settlement, to be paid over a period of sixty-two years. Commented one outraged American newspaper, "Supposing in 1917 we had said to Europe, 'Sure, we'll come across—in about sixty-two years.' " Vice President Calvin Coolidge had only one tight-lipped comment about the Allies' obligation: "They hired the money, didn't they?"

The French argued that the war loans were actually credits spent in the United States that had provided Americans with a wartime and postwar prosperity. Hadn't America emerged from the war powerful and rich, the land untouched, owning more than half the gold in the world?

"American resentment against France is equalled by French resentment against the United States," Tardieu declared, blaming the Americans for "an undeniable lack of understanding and of good will." A Parisian newspaper angrily published a political cartoon showing the ghost of a dead French *poilu* asking America, "In your accounting, have you included my blood and that of my brother soldiers?"

How were they supposed to pay back the loans, the French demanded, when America imposed a high tariff to keep out French imports? France didn't have enough gold, and America wouldn't accept payment in goods. Washington, furthermore, refused to let France exact heavy reparations from Germany.

The former allies were alienated further in December, 1921, at the Washington Naval Disarmament Conference, at which American officials accused France of being "the only nation which refused to disarm." Political observer Mark Sullivan wrote, "France has acted badly. . . . The part she has played cannot and will not be forgiven." American editorials pointed out bitingly that if the French could afford a large navy, they could also afford to pay their debts to the United States.

The French press lashed back at American unwillingness to recognize that France needed a large navy to link and protect its colonial empire of sixty million people.

In 1922 Clemenceau visited America in an effort to keep Franco-American relations from deteriorating still further. He received a warm personal welcome, but winced at sharp criticism in the press. *The Nation*, bitter over Wilson's failure at Versailles, told him, "You say you want more than America's money. You want our hearts and souls. But, M. Clemenceau, France had our hearts and souls, and more than that. It is not easy to give again that which has been offered once and tossed aside with contempt. You accepted our money and our men, but our ideals, our hopes, our dreams and visions . . . you refused. . . . Our people . . . are left with a sense of bruised disillusionment."

Stung, Clemenceau told Americans, "If we had known that we were to be left in the lurch by . . . American indifference, we should not have signed the armistice. . . . You came too late and you withdrew too soon." He later wrote an angry public reply to Coolidge's demands for French concessions in lieu of the defaulted loans. "France is not for sale," he declared, "even to her friends."

He charged that Americans did not recognize that they had already been paid by a "bank account" for three years before they entered the war: "Come to our villages and read the endless lists of their dead and make comparisons, if you will. Was this not a 'bank account,' the loss of this . . . youth?"

Disillusionment with war swept both countries. In 1928 French Premier Aristide Briand invited Secretary of State Frank B. Kellogg to co-sponsor a world pact pledging all nations to use arbitration instead of war to settle their disputes. The Kellogg-Briand Pact, eventually signed by over sixty nations, brought about voluntary arbitration of some international quarrels, but it lacked enforcement machinery.

Finally, three signatories made the Pact absolutely worthless by violating it—Japan by invading Manchuria in 1931, Italy and Germany by Fascist aggression during the Thirties. Breach of the Pact was the legal basis for the war crimes trials that took place at Nuremberg after World War II.

When the grim, sacrificial war years came to an end in 1919, Americans flung themselves into the "Roaring Twenties." Provincialism, materialism and shallow frivolity characterized the nation's "return to normalcy" under Harding and Coolidge.

Despite strained Franco-American political relations, France was still attractive to various classes of Americans. In the spirit of "whooping it up," war-enriched tourists sought to frolic in Paris. Socialites, disdaining the vulgarity of *nouveaux riches* diversions at home, went to the French Riviera to gamble, sun-bathe and fraternize with European aristocracy.

Also in flight from the vulgarity of "Babbittry" that had overtaken the United States were thousands of artists, writers and musicians who flocked to Paris, the cultural center of the Western world. Young expatriates also found postwar living in Paris much cheaper and more rewarding. For $1,600 a year or less they could enjoy French cooking, wine, life in a beautiful city, access to many of the world's greatest art treasures, and the companionship of sophisticated and creative people from Europe and America.

Great writers, artists and musicians of the time gathered at the Paris salon of Philadelphia-born Gertrude Stein. "America is my country," she declared, "but Paris is my home town." Among the American writers who came to postwar Paris were Ernest Hemingway, F. Scott Fitzgerald, John Dos Passos, Dorothy Parker, e.e. cummings, Ezra Pound, Archibald MacLeish, Stephen Vincent Benet and T.S. Eliot. Composers included George Gershwin, Virgil Thompson and Aaron Copland, who declared, "I wanted to go where the new music was, to Debussy, to Ravel." Among the painters were Thomas Hart Benson and Grant Wood.

Gertrude Stein explained why Paris had become the mecca for so many gifted and intelligent Americans: "Paris was where the twentieth century was." Like dissenters of our own time, the expatriates rejected the values of the American majority of their day. "It was impossible to be creative," explained an American artist who left Cleveland for Paris," in an atmosphere of narrow-minded, conservative Puritanism."

The "Bohemians," as they were called, had an American colony on the Left Bank of Paris, the equivalent of New York's Greenwich Village of that day. Rebellious young Americans from the midwest enjoyed the freedom and fun of the Latin Quarter as they studied art, music and writing. Gertrude Stein called them "the lost generation."

An earlier view of the French began to reappear. France was again seen as an amusing country of frivolity, gaiety, artists and sexual sophistication—a place where one went to enjoy himself, quite different from the France of Lafayette, Napoleon or Foch.

There was, however, one large group of Americans who went to France in a serious mood. Parents whose sons had died in Normandy made pilgrimages to the battlefields and America's military cemetaries, where 30,000 dead had been buried beside the French dead in the ravaged soil of France. This group was so large that the U.S. War Department sent Major Dwight D. Eisenhower to Paris for a year to prepare a government guidebook to the battlefields for them. The Eisenhower apartment on the Quai d'Auteuil became "a home away from home" for army people in Paris, who renamed their square "Place Eisenhower" and the Mirabeau Bridge there "Pont Mamie" after the major's popular wife.

Eisenhower, roaming the battlefields to prepare the guidebook, studied them with an eye toward military strategy if the Germans ever attacked again. He could scarcely imagine that this responsibility would actually rest upon his own shoulders a quarter of a century later.

12

France in Chains

THE world depression ushered in by the Wall Street crash of 1929 precipitated a turbulent struggle between Right and Left factions in France. The French Left won in 1934 by forming a Popular Front coalition government under Premier Léon Blum. Watching these developments from Washington, President Franklin D. Roosevelt was sensitive to the threat posed to France's democracy by her two Fascist neighbors.

He used the occasion of the centennial of Lafayette's death to sound a subtle warning to Hitler and Mussolini in a speech to Congress in 1934 that stressed traditional Franco-American ties: "The people of this Nation . . . cherish [Lafayette's] memory more than that of any citizen of a foreign country. . . . Many generations later, more than two million American boys . . . went to France . . . repaying a debt of gratitude to preserve those fundamentals of liberty and democracy to which . . . he had dedicated his life."

In 1936, ignoring this veiled warning, Hitler and Mussolini forged the Rome-Berlin Axis aimed against the democracies. Hitler sent his army to occupy the German Rhineland, demilitarized by the Versailles Treaty, correctly guessing that France would do no more than protest. He and Mussolini then completed the Fascist encirclement of France by helping General Francisco Franco to overthrow Republican Spain.

Roosevelt found himself in a dilemma similar to Wilson's in 1914. He understood the new German threat to democracy, but his power to make countermoves was checked by the now strongly isolationist sentiment of the American people. French leaders also recognized the danger, but were afraid to challenge the Fascist powers without an American or British alliance, especially since France had been weakened by a dropping birth rate, inflation, strikes and unemployment. (While both governments stood aside and allowed Fascism to triumph in Spain, thousands of American idealists enlisted in an International Brigade of volunteers. They reached Spain from France, where the government shut its eyes as French guides took them over the border across the Pyrenees. After Franco's victory, Republican refugees were given asylum by the sympathetic French in Brittany.)

The triumphant march of Fascism continued through 1938. At Munich, Hitler bluffed Prime Minister Neville Chamberlain (nicknamed "Neville J'aime-Berlin" by anti-Fascist Frenchmen) and French Premier Edouard Daladier into appeasing him by letting him take over Czechoslovakia.

The now alarmed French government sent a secret mission to the United States to buy fighter-bombers. Isolationists in

Roosevelt's Cabinet sought to block negotiations, but the President ordered a secret demonstration of Douglas Aircraft attack bombers for the mission. One of the planes crashed. A Senate inquiry opened when one of the passengers killed was identified as a member of the French Air Ministry.

General Henry Arnold, Air Corps Chief of Staff, testified that he had arranged the demonstration reluctantly, at Roosevelt's insistence. He denied that the War Department had authorized it. Irritated, the President told him privately, "If some members of the Air Corps don't get on the team when testifying before Congress, they may find themselves in Guam!"

But Secretary of the Treasury Henry Morgenthau also testified that the military plane deal with France had been authorized by the President. Republican Senators accused Roosevelt of committing the United States to war through secret diplomacy. The planes were delivered to France when Hitler's persistent acts of aggression led Congress to amend America's neutrality acts to aid France and Britain.

On September 1, 1939, Hitler invaded Poland, which had a defense pact with England and France. They were forced to declare war, and World War II began.

"This nation will remain a neutral nation," Roosevelt declared in a fireside chat, "but I cannot ask that every American remain neutral in thought as well."

The French knew then that they were in a race with time: would Roosevelt be able to persuade the American people that the cause of France and Britain was once more their own before Hitler's military blitz swept across Western Europe?

(In October, scientist Albert Einstein wrote a letter to Roosevelt informing him that it was now possible to develop an atomic bomb—"through the work of Joliot in France as well as Fermi and Szilard in America.")

For almost seven months, Frenchmen crouched behind their presumably impregnable Maginot Line of fortresses, while Hitler organized his forces for a lightning offensive. In May, 1940, the German army struck. Sweeping around the Maginot Line to seize Belgium, it rolled into northern France. A Nazi tank blitzkrieg drove a wedge between French and British forces, forcing a British evacuation at Dunkirk. Six days later, on June 10th, Mussolini hastily sought a share of war spoils by his own declaration of war against the battered democracies. "The hand that held the dagger," Roosevelt said angrily, "has struck it into the back of its neighbor."

Prime Minister Paul Reynaud, who had succeeded Daladier, wanted to assign the defense of France in her hour of desperation to a dynamic young general, Charles de Gaulle. De Gaulle had argued vainly against pinning France's defenses on a stationary Maginot Line. A student of Patton's tank tactics in World War I, he had pleaded for armored divisions capable of lightning strikes against the enemy. Ironically, the French General Staff had refused to listen; Hitler's generals had.

Because de Gaulle was then relatively unknown to the French people, however, Reynaud was compelled to turn instead to two old heroes of World War I. Marshal Henri Philippe Pétain became Minister of State, and General Maxime Weygand Commander of the French army. Both men saw no other recouse for France but to seek an armistice on Germany's terms.

Pétain and Weygand were not simply pessimistic; they were

Rightists who hated the Third Republic. By letting it fall, they could bring about a new Right-wing France modeled after Franco's Spain or—Weygand's choice—a new French monarchy.

When Reynaud realized the extent of their defeatist policy, he appealed privately to President Roosevelt for immediate aid to save France. "From this moment onward," he pleaded, "France cannot continue to fight unless American intervention arrives to reverse the situation, making an Allied victory certain. The only chance to save the French nation . . . is today to throw in the scales the weight of American strength."

He pointed out, "It is also the only chance to keep Hitler, after having destroyed France, then England, from attacking America. . . . I know that a declaration of war does not depend on you alone. But . . . at this grave hour in our history, as in yours, [if you fail to help us] you will then see France go down like a drowning man and disappear, after having thrown a last look toward the land of liberty where she sought salvation."

Embarrassed, Roosevelt replied, "In these hours which are so heart-rending for the French people and yourself, I send you the assurances of my utmost sympathy." He promised that as long as the French continued fighting, the United States would send them supplies, but added cautiously, "I know you will understand that these statements carry with them no implication of military commitments. Only the Congress can make such commitments."

De Gaulle urged Reynaud not to give up hope. "In this world conflict it is only a matter of time before the United States intervenes on Britain's side," he predicted. "As to the

An interior view of the Maginot Line, a series of defensive fortifications built before World War II to protect the eastern border of France. The line is named after André Maginot, French Minister of War during the 1920s.

FRENCH EMBASSY PRESS AND INFORMATION DIVISION

Russians, I prophesy . . . they will join in before the Americans." But it was already too late.

The Germans, brushing aside light French resistance, headed for Paris. Reynaud was forced to declare Paris an open city and move the seat of the French government to Bordeaux. But with Pétain and Weygand already determined to make an armistice, Reynaud was compelled to resign. On June 16th, Pétain became the new head of the French government. Asking Germany for terms, he surrendered France five days later.

In the tiny village of Montoire, Pétain met Hitler in a railroad car—the same car in which Germany had been forced to surrender to France in 1918. Shaking hands with Hitler, he announced, "It is with honor and in order to maintain French unity . . . that I embark today on a course of collaboration."

One stubborn French general refused to accept the legality of Pétain's surrender, denouncing it as an act of treason. Charles de Gaulle, who had been sent to London by Reynaud, found Prime Minister Winston Chruchill ready to give him every help in keeping France in the war. De Gaulle formed the Free French National Committee, broadcasting appeals from London for continued French resistance.

"Is the defeat permanent? No!" he assured his anguished people. "For France is not alone. . . . She can, like England, make unlimited use of the immense industry of the United States. . . . I, General de Gualle, now in London, invite French officers and soldiers . . . to put themselves in contact with me. Whatever happens, the flame of French resistance must not and will not go out. . . . I, General de Gaulle, French soldier and leader, speak in the name of France!"

Meanwhile, under the terms of the German armistice, the

Henri Philippe Pétain was appointed Minister of State by French Prime Minister Paul Reynaud and was later premier of Vichy France.

FRENCH EMBASSY PRESS AND INFORMATION DIVISION

Nazis occupied the northern half of France, including Paris. The southern half was put under Pétain in Vichy, with pro-Nazi Pierre Laval as Vice Premier. This puppet dictatorship controlled the French army and navy in France's overseas empire, keeping them from going over to de Gaulle and his Free French. The Vichy regime was also required to collaborate by recruiting workers for German war industry, and by supplying Nazi military and civilian needs.

"The Americans won't be ready for four years," Pétain told his Colonial Minister. "It's going to be hard. We shall have to pocket our pride. Our contract with the Germans is for 'present circumstances.' Well, the victor always calls the tune." He permitted the Nazis to ship French Jews to German extermination camps. An appalled French general told Pétain that he was "dishonoring our uniform."

"Go to hell," replied Pétain.

Another complex key figure in Pétain's Vichy government was Admiral Jean Francois Darlan. He controlled the French fleet, and was determined to keep it out of German hands, by scuttling it if necessary. Yet he was not above fraternizing with and flattering the Nazis. He expressed his gratitude to Hitler for not "obliterating France from the map of the world," and advised officials in France's North African territories to cooperate with the Germans.

Liberal Americans rallied enthusiastically to de Gaulle's cause when he appeared in Brazzaville, capital of Free French Africa, in October, 1940, and declared:

"There exists no longer a truly French government. In point of fact, the body that sits at Vichy and that pretends to bear that name is unconstitutional and in subjection to the invader. . . . It is necessary therefore for a new power to assume the burden of directing the French war effort. Events impose this sacred duty upon me. . . . I will exercise my powers in the name of France and only to defend it."

Roosevelt, nevertheless, felt that prudence required him to maintain cordial relations with the Vichy government in order to keep the French overseas army and navy bases in North Africa out of German hands. In the hope of persuading Pétain to co-operate secretly against Hitler, Roosevelt sent Admiral William Leahy as Ambassador to Vichy, instructing him to "cultivate as close relations with Marshal Pétain as possible."

Leahy reported to the President that Pétain "gave me a definite impression of vigor and strength of character, and of personal appreciation of the friendly attitude of America." He added further that Pétain's word was law, "and nothing can be accomplished if he opposes it." De Gaulle, Leahy said, was a "self-appointed leader of a so-called resistance movement . . . lusting for power." De Gaulle's American supporters were dismissed as "a group of Jews and Communists."

The naive Leahy scarcely realized that he was playing into Hitler's hands by parroting Vichy-Berlin propaganda.

Churchill, who supported de Gaulle, recognized that he represented French feeling far more than Pétain did. But the British leader was nevertheless exasperated by the haughty manner of "*le grand Charles*," who declared emphatically, "I *am* France." Churchill had been forced to roar, "No, General, you are *not* France, however much you claim to be!"

Unwilling to make a single concession to expediency, de Gaulle demanded, "What would have happened to France if Joan of Arc, Danton or Clemenceau had been willing to com-

Pétain (left) and Admiral Darlan (right), Foreign Minister of Vichy, during a parade. Darlan, an enigmatic man who negotiated at various times with both the Allies and the Nazis, was assassinated in Algiers in December, 1942, by a French anti-Fascist.

FRENCH EMBASSY PRESS AND INFORMATION DIVISION

promise?" This remark, reported to Roosevelt, led the President to mock him unfairly as having claimed to be a modern Joan of Arc.

Roosevelt's refusal to take de Gaulle seriously was encouraged not only by Leahy at Vichy, but also by Secretary of State Cordell Hull. "The President and I had no hesitation in continuing diplomatic relations with the Pétain government," Hull related later, "while waiting to see what its ultimate policy would be. . . . The Pétain government was a legal government."

Roosevelt sent Vichy civilian supplies, whenever Churchill grudgingly consented, in the hope of stiffening Pétain's resistance to German demands. Hull believed, "We could encourage the French people by convincing them we are still with them." He hoped that eventually Weygand could be persuaded to switch allegiance to the British.

But this policy of appeasement only convinced the French people that America supported Vichy. The French Resistance, which saw de Gaulle's Free French movement as the chief hope of liberating France, was discouraged.

Leahy also influenced Hull and Roosevelt by his private contempt for the French army. In his memoirs he wrote, "To me, the 'magnificent French army' was only pretty fast on its feet. It almost got away—by running." By not pointing out that Germany's victory stemmed directly from the military mistakes of the generals now in power in Vichy—against de Gaulle's advice—Leahy unfairly and unwisely prejudiced Roosevelt's dealings with de Gaulle.

The President was led to take a condescending view of France as a nation. "In more pessimistic moments I have of necessity come to believe [the worst] . . . about France and the French future," he once wrote, "yet I always say to myself that in previous [crises] France has always snapped out of it. This optimism, I must frankly confess, has little foundation." He blamed all Frenchmen for France's swift collapse under the onslaught of the Nazi war machine.

In the fall of 1940 Weygand argued with Pétain that Vichy should concede the Germans nothing more than the surrender their treaty called for. Pétain angrily exiled him to Algiers on the pretext of needing him there to crush the Free French movement in North Africa. Weygand had a close friend in diplomat Robert Murphy, America's chief agent in the French colonies, who now persuaded Hull to support him as a possible future ally against Hitler. Yet Weygand had expressed the hope that England's neck would be "wrung like a chicken."

Roosevelt, thoroughly misguided by Leahy in Vichy, Hull in Washington, and Murphy in Algiers, tied American policy to the Vichy regime. The French people and most anti-Nazi Europeans, meanwhile, were rallying to de Gaulle.

The President wrote a personal letter of "sympathy and understanding" to Pétain in February, 1941, expressing hope for a "continuation of the free and independent France for which you have fought with such steadfast courage and determination." Delighted, Pétain was also pleased by Leahy's refusal to see any de Gaulle supporter, whom Leahy scorned in Pétain's own terms as "a traitor to his country."

Leahy even demanded that Churchill dump de Gaulle, insisting that this move "would go far in swinging the old soldier [Pétain] more toward the British camp." Hull was persuaded to soothe Pétain by asking Britain to ease its naval blockade of occupied France. Churchill refused, but backed down when Hull warned that Admiral Darlan would otherwise order the French fleet to oppose the Royal Navy.

American isolationism began to crumble under the threat of Hitler's dazzling military triumphs. Roosevelt was now able to persuade Congress to appropriate a $7 billion Lend-Lease Act to make America "the great arsenal of democracy," arming and supplying Britain. The news reached Churchill at his home estate of Chequers, where de Gaulle was a guest. He woke up the French leader at 4:00 A.M. and danced around his bed chortling, "Now we'll get the tools!"

It was good news for de Gaulle, too, even though Roosevelt and Hull refused to deal with him. Churchill would now be able to release more equipment to the Free French. De Gaulle told the British leader thoughtfully, "I'm sure the United States will eventually enter the war."

Pétain named Admiral Darlan Foreign Minister of Vichy and second in command, above Laval. A cynical opportunist, Darlan had only one guiding principle—to end up on the winning side. As of early 1941 he was convinced that would be Germany. Leahy assured Roosevelt that the United States could sway Darlan if they offered him more than the Nazis did.

In May, when German Field Marshal Erwin Rommel attacked British forces in Cairo, Darlan supplied him with hundreds of French trucks. Meeting Hitler at Berchesgaden, Darlan begged him to accept Vichy France as a full partner in the Rome-Berlin Axis. Pétain declared in a radio broadcast, "Frenchmen you have learned of Admiral Darlan's talks with Hitler. I approved the principle of the meeting."

Roosevelt now began to realize that his Vichy policy had been a serious miscalculation. If Darlan and Weygand turned French North Africa over to the Nazis, Hitler would have the Atlantic fortress of Dakar—only five hours by bomber to Washington. "The war is approaching the brink of the Western Hemisphere," he commented, worried. "It is coming very close to home."

Even now Leahy persisted in opposing de Gaulle, finding "no indication in occupied France that the self-styled 'leader of French resistance' has any important numerical following." He made that report to Washington from Vichy, without once setting foot anywhere in occupied France.

In June, 1941, Hitler fulfilled de Gaulle's prophecy that "he will repeat Napoleon's mistake." Having signed a non-aggression pact with Stalin, Hitler suddenly violated it by ordering an invasion of the Soviet Union. Russia's danger galvanized the French Communists who, until then, had not been active in the French underground Resistance movement.

Now the whole French Left—Communists, Socialists, radicals of all parties—sprang into action to harass the German occupation forces with sabotage, acts of terror and guerrilla raids. Many units fought in the name of de Gaulle and the Free French, spreading their activities into Vichy France. The French people gave them enthusiastic support.

Pétain was soon forced to admit on radio, "From several regions of France I have sensed for some weeks the rising of an evil wind. Worry is winning minds and doubt is seizing souls. The authority of my government is being questioned."

In June, de Gaulle rushed envoy René Pleven to Washington to urge Hull to switch recognition from Vichy to the Free

French. Hull refused even to see Pleven, who reported that Vichy propaganda had hoodwinked Leahy, Murphy, Hull and Roosevelt into believing de Gaulle had no support in France.

"We must convince the Americans," Pleven summed up their dilemma, "that Free France is the France they have loved."

13

*The Roosevelt–
de Gaulle Feud*

LEAHY advised Roosevelt that Churchill supported de Gaulle because the Free French leader was actually "a paid British agent." The President was further assured that "all Frenchmen" hated the British: "Practically the entire population . . . looks only to America for its salvation."

But Leahy became disenchanted with Pétain when the British mounted an offensive in North Africa against Rommel, and Hitler demanded more help there from Weygand. The French general resisted. Pétain, fearful of Hitler's wrath, stripped Weygand of all military powers despite Leahy's protests.

"It seems necessary to abandon all hope," the disillusioned American admiral now wrote Roosevelt gloomily, "of trying to give some backbone to a jellyfish. . . . This is an appropriate time to consider a complete revision of American policy." But in North Africa Murphy still championed Vichy, warning that if the United States cut off aid to Pétain, he would have no other choice but to turn to the Nazis.

194

In September, 1941, de Gaulle organized the French National Committee in London, a cabinet-in-exile of ministers of various shades of political opinion, to serve as a provisional governing body for France. Hull ignored the FNC, but it quickly won recognition from Britain, the Soviet Union and refugee governments whose countries Hitler had overrun.

December 7, 1941, brought electrifying news to Europe.

The United States plunged into the war after Pearl Harbor. De Gaulle now predicted to his Chief of Intelligence, "Now the war is definitely won! And after it the future has two phases in store for us: the first will be the rescue of Germany by the Allies; as for the second, I fear it may be a great war between the Russians and the Americans—and that war, Passy, the Americans will lose!"

In an obvious bid for recognition, he now offered Washington a "Lafayette Escadrille" of French fliers to aid the American air force, echoing the American volunteers who had flown for France in the early years of World War I. His gesture was coldly rejected as "technically unfeasible." For despite the fact that America was now at war with Germany, Hull continued to ignore de Gaulle and deal with Pétain. This was an intolerable affront to the French leader whom Churchill had told, "You embody the hope of millions of Frenchmen and Frenchwomen."

He now wrote Churchill angrily, "I am fearful of the mistaken impression that this sort of public preference accorded by the government of the United States to those responsible for capitulation and guilty of collaboration will produce [in France]. . . . It does not seem right to me that, in war, the prize should be awarded to the apostles of dishonor."

Relations between de Gaulle and Roosevelt deteriorated steadily. In the President's eyes, the French general was petty, self-serving, ambitious for power, ridiculously haughty and arrogant. In de Gaulle's eyes, Roosevelt was supercilious and patronizing.

Further clashes lay ahead. Stalin kept pleading for a second front to be opened by the Allied invasion of northern France, to ease the pressure of the German offensive against Russia. But the American Chiefs of Staff rejected this plan as too difficult and costly. They decided instead to seize North Africa, from which they could invade first Italy, then France's more vulnerable southern coast.

"Operation Torch" counted on Washington's support of Vichy; this would keep the 200,000-man French army in the North African colonies from opposing Allied landings. Roosevelt's advisers urged him to keep the plans and date of the invasion secret from de Gaulle, who could be expected to oppose any deals with Vichy forces in the French colonies.

Although Leahy was now disgusted with Vichy, he wrote to the President, "Our British friends seem to believe that the body of the entire people of France is strongly behind de Gaulle, whereas according to all my information . . . more than ninety-five percent . . . are not de Gaullists and would not follow him. This fact leads straight to our plans about North Africa and our omission of de Gaulle's co-operation in that connection."

Roosevelt sought a French general of sufficient stature to make Operation Torch appear to be an act of liberation to the French in the colonies so that they would not resist the Allied landings. Churchill insisted that only de Gaulle had the necessary prestige and popular support. Roosevelt replied that all of his advisers assured him most Frenchmen detested de Gaulle. Besides, Hull considered de Gaulle "desperately temperamental," with little political acumen.

Weygand was offered the job of French leader for Operation Torch. He not only refused but revealed the plan to Pétain, who angrily let Leahy know he would defend French territory against any foreign power. Did that mean Americans, too? "It means anybody—including Americans!" Pétain snapped. The problem was thrown in Murphy's lap.

Murphy selected General Henri Giraud, who had taken an oath of loyalty and obedience to Pétain and who despised de Gaulle. He had some popular support because he had been captured in the Battle of France, had refused to co-operate with the Germans and had escaped. His daughter had been jailed and killed in a concentration camp. Murphy arranged for Giraud to be spirited out of Vichy France by submarine, then flown to Gilbraltar by seaplane to consult with General Dwight Eisenhower, who was now Supreme Commander of the Allied Forces.

De Gaulle was kept in the dark about Operation Torch until after the Allies landed in North Africa. British Chief of Staff Hastings Ismay told him, "The Americans made us keep it secret from you because the intervention of the Free French would complicate everything. I understand your bitterness. Overcome it."

"I hope the Vichy people throw them into the sea," de Gaulle replied. "They can't break into France like burglars!" His Free French newspaper in London, *La Marsellaise*, declared, "France has suffered an immense wrong. The occupation by our American allies of a land which cost us so much blood . . . damages her honor."

Cooling off, however, de Gaulle rose to the occasion with an inspiring broadcast to the French people. "Here is the great moment!" he cried. "Here is the hour for good sense and courage!" He addressed the North African army: "Rise up and help our Allies. Join them without reservation. The France which is fighting makes this appeal to you. Don't worry about names or fame. Only one thing counts—saving France!"

Pétain now showed his colors. "It is with stupor and grief that I learned during the night of the aggression of your troops in North Africa," he wired Roosevelt. ". . . France and her honor are at stake. We are attacked. We shall defend ourselves. This is the order I am giving."

If Roosevelt still had any doubts about his blunder in coddling the Vichy government, they were gone forever after November, 1942, when French guns in North Africa blazed at the Americans who had come as liberators.

On the eve of Operation Torch, Eisenhower flew to Gibraltar to direct operations as 400,000 Allied troops ploughed their way toward landings at Casablanca, Oran and Algiers. At British headquarters a visitor was ushered in to him.

"General Giraud has arrived," the French general announced himself dramatically, "and is ready to assume command of all operations." He handed Eisenhower a letter from Murphy promising Giraud charge of operations in French North Africa. Astonished by Giraud's expectations, Eisenhower explained tactfully that his role was simply to bring French troops there over to the Allied side.

"*Non!* Giraud cannot accept less than *supreme command!*"

But eventually he agreed to go to Algiers, where Allied landings had met no opposition. At Oran and Casablanca, invading troops were encountering fierce resistance. "Existing French sentiment here," Eisenhower cabled Washington, "does not remotely agree with prior calculations." He ordered all invasion areas showered with leaflets urging the French to co-operate with Giraud.

Soon after Giraud's arrival in Algiers, General Mark Clark radioed Eisenhower that Vichy officials and generals there had denounced Giraud as a traitor to Pétain, forcing him to flee into hiding. Only the authority of Admiral Darlan, Vichy's Commander in Chief, was recognized. He "happened" to be in Algiers, Clark reported, and was ready to make a deal. Darlan's price was Allied recognition of him as the supreme authority in North Africa; Giraud could command the military forces, but only under him.

Darlan, obviously, no longer expected the Nazis to win.

Eisenhower agreed to the deal to save time and lives. He hoped it would mean he could add French divisions to the Allied armies and perhaps even win over the French fleet. Hadn't Washington ordered him to co-operate with *any* French government in control of North Africa? All French opposition to Operation Torch collapsed, and the Allies' North African base was secured.

Eisenhower was stunned when a storm of criticism blew up in the American and British press over the Darlan affair. He was accused of making a notorious Nazi collaborator an ally, thereby seriously damaging the principles for which the war was being fought. Murphy told him that de Gaulle was on his way to Algiers for a showdown, but advised Eisenhower to pay no attention because de Gaulle was supported by only about ten percent of the French people.

"Roosevelt," de Gaulle complained bitterly, "is blinded by Murphy's reports." When the Free French leader arrived in Algiers, he was greeted by a cheering thong of over a hundred thousand people. Murphy, impressed, congratulated him by observing, "Quite an enormous crowd."

The tall general replied frostily, "They represent, *monsieur,* some of your ten percent!"

On reflection, Eisenhower felt that de Gaulle deserved an apology for the shabby way he had been treated by the Allies. He went to see the French leader at his hotel.

"You were originally described to me unfavorably," he said candidly. "Now I realize that was an error. For the coming battle I must have your assistance. So I've come to ask you for it."

Deeply moved, de Gaulle grasped his hand. "You are a *man!*" he declared fervently. "For you know how to say, 'I was wrong!' "

The opportunistic Darlan co-operated with the Americans in Algiers, but at the same time hedged his bets by secretly ordering his commanders in Tunisia to co-operate with the Germans. He also permitted the French navy to fire on occasion upon Allied shipping, but never at Fascist ships. Newspaper reporters, moreover, discovered that he was enforcing Fascist laws in Morocco and allowing the brutalization of political prisoners in concentration camps. De Gaulle wanted him removed.

Eisenhower found himself on the horns of an embarrassing political dilemma. How could he ensure North African co-operation of the Vichy French without Darlan? Yet how could he condone Darlan's despicable conduct?

In Vichy, meanwhile, a now almost senile Pétain had broken off relations with the United States over the invasion of the French colonies. He nursed a bitter hatred of de Gaulle, calling all who supported him the "enemies of France." Pétain's failure to keep his North African bases out of Allied hands infuriated Hitler. In November, 1942, Nazi troops marched into Vichy France, ending all pretense of Vichy's sovereignty. Pétain was no longer a puppet, but a captive.

Acting in Pétain's name, Darlan ordered French crews at Toulon to scuttle the French fleet to keep it out of Nazi hands. He also announced that the French army in North Africa would now join the Allies in fighting Germany for the liberation of France. Vastly relieved, Eisenhower reported to Roosevelt, "Civil governors, military leaders and naval commanders agree that only one man has an obvious right to assume the Marshal's mantle in North Africa. He is Darlan."

Even Churchill explained to Parliament, "Many Frenchmen who admire General de Gaulle . . . nevertheless regard him as a man who has rebelled against the authority of the French state [as symbolized by] Marshal Pétain. . . . Now all this may seem very absurd in our minds. But . . . the Marshal is acting under the duress of the invading Hun, and . . . Darlan is still carrying out his truest wishes."

Sarcastically, Roosevelt wrote to Churchill his solution to the French puzzle: "Place Admiral Darlan, General Giraud, and a de Gaulle representative in one room alone, and then give the government of the occupied territory to the man who comes out."

De Gaulle denounced Roosevelt's recognition of Darlan as the spokesman for France. Hull replied blandly, "The French people will continue, I am sure, to be grateful to us for our policies." At that de Gaulle exploded.

"The United States can pay traitors," he said, "but not with the honor of France. . . . I do not share President Roosevelt's opinion when he explains that it is a question of avoiding bloodshed and implies that anything goes. As for myself, I will not lend myself, either directly or indirectly, to this sickening saga. What remains of the honor of France will stay intact in *my* hands!"

Angry American liberals rallied to his cause. Seeking to placate them, Roosevelt promised, "The present arrangement in North and West Africa is only a temporary expedient, justified solely by the stress of battle."

The President recognized that his treatment of the Free French was inconsistent with his otherwise liberal views on all other foreign policy matters. But he was a stubborn man, too proud to admit that he had been badly mistaken in his judgment of Charles de Gaulle. Even though Leahy now admitted that de Gaulle *did* represent popular French sentiment, Roosevelt only replied, "I am a pig-headed Dutchman, Bill. . . . You can't change my mind." The President was shocked, however, when Darlan, instead of transferring the French fleet to the Allies, ordered it scuttled.

Roosevelt began to have second thoughts about the wisdom of continuing to support a Vichy-tainted French leader. He realized that a liberated French people would never accept a Darlan or a Giraud at the head of an interim government. Only de Gaulle's hands were clean of collaboration with the enemy; only he had held up the banner of the Fighting French; only he was respected and admired by his people.

But the President could not forgive de Gaulle's exasperatingly haughty manner. Far from expressing appreciation for the American liberation of the French colonies, de Gaulle made it clear that he suspected American intentions. How could they be considered liberated as long as they continued to be governed by the American military instead of by the Free French?

Roosevelt had even snapped at a de Gaulle emissary, André Philip, that until France itself was freed, "the sole decision as to what, if any Frenchmen would administer the liberated territory was a matter solely for this government to determine."

"We are not a colony," Philip replied stiffly. "The American army will never make us accept the authority of traitors!"

On Christmas Eve, 1942, a young French anti-Fascist, disgusted by the failure of the American landings to end Vichyism in North Africa, assassinated Darlan. Eisenhower, Churchill and even Roosevelt were secretly relieved to have the Vichy admiral out of the way. Eisenhower wanted to replace him with de Gaulle, but his advisers warned that the French military in North Africa would never consent. Nor would Roosevelt. So Giraud was given Darlan's powers.

To Eisenhower's dismay, Giraud proved even more undemocratic than Darlan. He arrested and held without trial Free French supporters who had helped the Allied landings. Pressured to remove Algeria's pro-Fascist governor general, Giraud replaced him with an ex-Vichy minister infamous for his torture of prisoners.

Eisenhower despaired of finding a French general acceptable to Washington who was not tainted with the spirit of Fascism.

14

"I Am France!"

THE nub of Eisenhower's difficulties, of course, was the refusal of Roosevelt to accept de Gaulle's claim to be the leader of Free France, despite the fact that there was no other French leader of stature who could truly make that claim. De Gaulle, on his part, was angry at Roosevelt for refusing to treat him as an equal ally who could speak for France. Echoes of ancient Franco-American suspicion, and the inevitable misunderstanding on both sides, marked the conflict of wills between the two world leaders.

Allied prospects brightened when the Russians won a great victory at Stalingrad, and Field Marshal Bernard Montgomery began chasing Rommel back across the hot African sands.

In January, 1943, Roosevelt and Churchill held a meeting at Casablanca, Morocco, to which F.D.R. brought Eisenhower and Giraud. Eisenhower and Churchill wanted de Gaulle to be invited also, but Roosevelt would not recognize the Free French as an equal ally. "I consider your position in French North Africa," he told Eisenhower, "to be that of a conqueror."

"But, Mr. President," Eisenhower said, "we did not defeat the French there. They *are* an ally. Acting on your orders, I negotiated an armistice with them. If we'd beaten them in battle, I certainly wouldn't have had to make those deals with Darlan and Giraud!"

Roosevelt was finally prevailed upon to invite de Gaulle tardily to the Casablanca Conference to try to work out a *modus vivendi* between him and Giraud. De Gaulle arrived without being accorded a formal reception or military honors, and was driven into a barbed wire compound surrounded by American troops.

"This is captivity!" he exploded. Meeting Giraud, he criticized him bitterly for agreeing to confer "in a barbed wire enclosure in the midst of foreigners."

He came face to face with Roosevelt for the first time in the President's villa. F.D.R., turning on his famous charm, sought to convince de Gaulle to accept American plans for France. But the President, de Gaulle later complained, was interested only in talking, not listening. Roosevelt failed to shake his determination that he, alone, represented the French people, and therefore could accept no position under Giraud —especially since Giraud was obviously taking orders from Washington.

"Only Frenchmen can decide the government of French territory," de Gaulle told Roosevelt. The President, angered, saved face by pretending at the end of the Conference that he

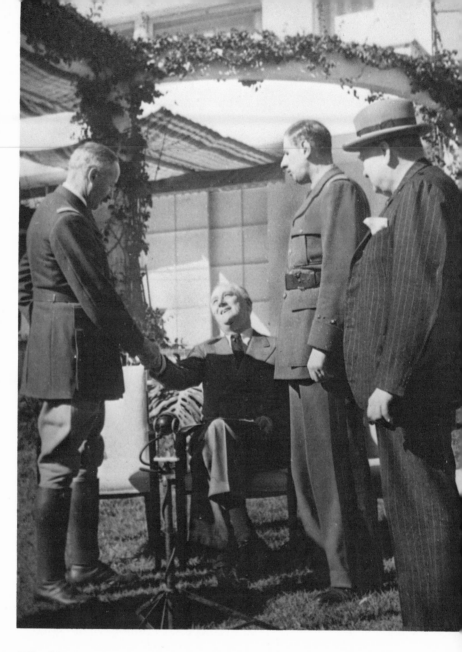

The historic meeting of (left to right) General Giraud, Roose-velt, de Gaulle, and Churchill at Casablanca in January, 1943. This was the first face to face meeting of de Gaulle and Roosevelt.

FRENCH EMBASSY PRESS AND INFORMATION DIVISION

had succeeded in resolving the thorny French question; he manipulated de Gaulle into shaking hands with Giraud for the benefit of news photographers. He wrote his son John that the conference had been a great success "and only General de Gaulle was a thoroughly bad boy." De Gaulle, in turn, reported to his deputies that he had given Roosevelt a lesson in reality. "I have the impression," he said, "that he discovered what Fighting France is."

De Gaulle also frustrated an attempt by F.D.R. to bait him into accepting the minor role of a French field commander. A Presidential envoy was sent to him with an offer to equip an Allied division and put it in combat under him.

"Then who is going to command France?" he asked acidly.

More and more his name became the symbol of French hope. In Paris the National Resistance Council, uniting all underground factions in France, recognized his leadership. Thousands of Giraud's troops in North Africa were deserting to the Fighting French forces. Wherever he appeared, crowds roared, *"Vive de Gaulle!"* His emblem, the Cross of Lorraine, was painted on French walls everywhere.

Once Churchill was asked about the greatest cross he had had to bear during the war. "The Cross of Lorraine," he sighed. British Foreign Minister Anthony Eden told de Gaulle bluntly, "Do you know you have caused us more trouble than all our other European allies put together?"

"I don't doubt it," de Gaulle replied. "France is a great power." But Roosevelt emphatically disagreed, considering de Gaulle's notions about the imperial greatness of his country absurd and obsolete. De Gaulle had angrily pointed out that the French were the leading power in North Africa.

"For the moment you are there," F.D.R. replied coldly. "But will you be there at the end of the act?"

De Gaulle feared that "the end of the act" would find "a new Vichy under American control" installed as the postwar government of France. That, he was convinced, would provoke a popular revolt led by the Communists. "The Americans will win the military war," he predicted, "but the political winner will be Stalin."

Organizing a National Committee of Liberation, he forced Giraud to join as a co-equal in power. Roosevelt ignored the NCL, telling Churchill, "I don't want to give de Gaulle a white horse on which he can ride into France and make himself master of a government there." When André Philip asked for recognition of the NCL, F.D.R. had a cynical reply:

"After our invasion, when elections have taken place, we shall know who is France. For the moment there is no France, so de Gaulle cannot speak in her name. I am not an idealist like Wilson. I am a realist. Darlan gave me North Africa: *vive Darlan!* If Laval gives me Paris, *vive Laval!* If Pétain gives me France, *vive le Maréchal!*"

But the President's options grew progressively narrower. De Gaulle, who skillfully maneuvered Giraud into a subordinate role in the NCL, became the only French leader outside France who could be welcomed back with invading Allied forces as a liberator. Roosevelt angrily ordered Chief of Staff George Marshall to stop supplying a French army in North Africa now controlled by "our prima donna."

But Marshall pointed out that Eisenhower still needed the French divisions for his operations in the Mediterranean. Frustrated, Roosevelt made it clear that when France was liberated, it would be administered by an Allied war council until Germany was defeated. De Gaulle was equally determined that as quickly as French territory was retaken, it would fall under French sovereignty. He was willing to co-operate fully with the Allies, but only as an independent equal.

In December, 1943, to display his authority and assure the French Resistance that he could be counted on to punish collaborationists as traitors, he arrested three notorious Vichy leaders in North Africa. But the three were now helping the Allies. Roosevelt angrily ordered Eisenhower to rescind their arrests. Eisenhower managed to avoid a showdown between F.D.R. and de Gaulle by persuading the French leader to postpone any trial of the collaborators until after the war.

It is interesting that in the spring of 1944, André Philip asked Hull to equip two French divisions so that de Gaulle could retake French Indo-China from the Japanese. Roosevelt wrote Hull sharply, "Indo-China should not go back to France . . . but be administered by an international trusteeship. France has had the country—thirty million inhabitants—for nearly a hundred years, and the people are worse off than they were at the beginning. . . . France has milked it for a hundred years. The people of Indo-China are entitled to something better than that!"

Meanwhile the Allied forces, with two French divisions, had fought their way up the Italian boot from North Africa. Now preparations began for the long-delayed Second Front—the invasion of northern France. De Gaulle insisted that the Allied Command discuss with his NCL the role to be played by the French army on D-Day. He suspected that Roosevelt planned to assign only a minor mission, distant from Paris, for his Free

French forces, to keep him from taking power.

When he was ignored, he angrily refused to let any more French troops be sent to Italy. Eisenhower sought to placate him by offering to assign the French army the task of invading France from the south, while British and American forces assaulted Normandy in the north. De Gaulle agreed, but only on condition that the Channel landings also include the French Second Armored Division under General Jacques Leclerc. He intended to give his own secret orders to Leclerc: to get to Paris speedily and take control before Communists in the Resistance seized power for themselves.

As Eisenhower returned to London to prepare for D-Day, de Gaulle bid him a fond adieu. Of all the Americans he knew, Eisenhower, generous and fair, was the only one he trusted. Eisenhower, in turn, appreciated the fact that de Gaulle, however prickly a cactus to handle, was still France's most popular hero. His great influence with the French people would assure their co-operation with the Allied military forces during the invasion of France, despite unavoidable suffering caused by a storm of death and destruction from Allied bombers.

In April, 1944, with preparations for D-Day well underway, de Gaulle learned that Washington had decided that French territory would be administered by an Allied Military Government of Occupied Territory (AMGOT) as it was recaptured. The Americans were already printing "Occupation francs" as legal currency. Outraged, de Gaulle once more forbade any further co-operation of Free French forces with the Allies.

He now defiantly changed the name of his NCL to "the Provisional Government of the French Republic." Churchill hastily conferred with him in London, and compromises were agreed upon which the Prime Minister then asked de Gaulle to go to Washington to propose to Roosevelt.

"Why do you think I have to submit to the authority of Roosevelt?" de Gaulle demanded. "The French government exists. I have nothing to ask of the United States or Great Britain in that area!"

Provoked, Churchill roared, "Every time I have to choose between you and Roosevelt, I'll choose Roosevelt!"

Eisenhower, as usual, acted as peacemaker. He filled in de Gaulle on all plans for D-Day and even let him read a speech Eisenhower planned to make to the people of occupied Europe on that occasion. The French leader noted that it called for French elections after liberation but was silent about de Gaulle and his Provisional Government of France.

"This is unacceptable," he said flatly.

Eisenhower appealed to Washington to give de Gaulle at least some share in the administration of liberated France. Roosevelt refused. Secretary of War Henry Stimson called the President a "tough customer," admitting that he himself was disappointed by "the degree of personal feeling which seemed to enter into the thinking of Mr. Roosevelt."

Eisenhower glumly realized that if de Gaulle refused to support AMGOT, it might be repudiated, even attacked, by the French Resistance. How could Eisenhower mount an all-out drive to crush Germany if he had to fight a disastrous civil war against the French Resistance and the Free French forces? The American general pleaded with de Gaulle to join him in a D-Day broadcast over BBC. The King of Norway, the Queen of the Netherlands, and the Prime Minister of Belgium would also urge their people to support the invading forces.

De Gaulle noted that he had been scheduled to speak last. He considered this arrangement not only insulting to France's prestige, but also a ploy to put him in the position of seeming to endorse the American plan for governing liberated France.

"I can assure you," Eisenhower promised, "that whatever apparent attitudes are imposed on me, I will recognize no French power other than your own in the practical sphere." This assurance exceeded Eisenhower's authority, but he firmly believed that a Supreme Commander in the field had the right to make his own decisions, regardless of prior orders, when an urgent military decision required it.

De Gaulle agreed to endorse the invasion, but only in a separate, later speech of his own. So while American and British troops were fighting on the beaches of Normandy, he called on his fellow countrymen to rally to them:

"The supreme battle has been joined . . . the battle for France. For the sons of France . . . the simple and sacred duty is to fight the enemy by every means in their power. . . . The orders given by the Government of France and by the leaders it has recognized must be obeyed."

He outwitted Roosevelt's attempt to keep him out of the liberated areas of France by slipping across the Channel to "inspect" the small strip of Normandy cleared of Germans. The French populace cheered wildly wherever he appeared. Returning to England, he confronted Eisenhower with a shrewd *fait accompli;* the Americans could take it or leave it.

"My staff has set up a provisional French government in Normandy," he told him. "We are now recruiting Free French forces to join your armies, General."

General de Gaulle landing in Normandy on June 14, 1944.
FRENCH EMBASSY PRESS AND INFORMATION DIVISION

"That's fine, General," Eisenhower sighed. The President would simply have to make the best of it. Indeed, Roosevelt had realized by now that he had no choice but to come to some kind of an understanding with the intransigent French general. So in July, 1944, he invited de Gaulle to Washington and sent his own plane to fly him there.

Welcomed at the airport with a seventeen-gun salute, de Gaulle responded in English with his first speech in the United States, stressing the traditional common interests of France and America. He met and talked with Hull and Leahy.

He caustically judged Hull to be "hampered by his slight understanding of anything not American, and by Roosevelt's interference in his domain." As for the former Ambassador to Vichy who was now the President's adviser, Leahy was considered to be "persisting in his prejudices."

After meeting Roosevelt again, de Gaulle noted privately, "It was difficult to contradict this artist, this seducer."

Now, at last, Roosevelt agreed to recognize de Gaulle's provisional French government as the temporary civilian authority in France until elections could be held. At the same time he reminded de Gaulle sharply that the shape of the post-war world would be decided by the realities of power, not sentimental considerations. But he painted a glowing picture of Allied plans for liberated France.

"It is evident," de Gaulle told the President coolly, "that if France is to regain her place in the world, she must count on no one but herself."

By mid-August the German armies were in full retreat from France, harassed by the guerrilla forces of the French Resistance whom Eisenhower said were "worth fifteen divisions." At the same time a Franco-American invasion force landed on the southern coast of France. The Vichy Government fell, and Pétain was whisked off to Germany.

On August 19th, Communist-led Partisans organized an uprising in Paris, hoping to seize power before Allied troops or de Gaulle's forces could reach the city. Fierce street battles broke out between civilians and Nazi troops. De Gaulle sped to Eisenhower's field headquarters.

French troops, he demanded, must be allowed to liberate Paris immediately. "Unless you agree, it will be clear to me that your State Department intends to keep me out of Paris until another French group establishes a government!"

"We are bypassing Paris," Eisenhower replied patiently, "because a battle in the city would kill thousands of civilians and cause terrible damage—no other reason!" Whether this was the whole truth, or whether he was acting on special orders from Roosevelt, has never been made clear.

"There is *already* fighting there!" de Gaulle pointed out. "If the Allied command delays too long in taking Paris, General, I *myself* shall order the Second Armored to do it!"

Eisenhower ordered Leclerc's division into Paris on August 23rd, and the Germans almost wiped them out. He had to reinforce them with other French and American units. De Gaulle's advisers urged him to rush to Paris at once and summon the National Assembly to confirm his government as the legal authority of France.

"I shall not do so," he replied scornfully. "*I* am the Government of France and need no one to confirm that fact!"

A half-mad Hitler ordered Paris burned but, after five days of fierce fighting, he surrendered the city on August 25th. Joy-

*General de Gaulle marching down the Champs Elysées on
August 25, 1944, in celebration of the liberation of Paris.*

FRENCH EMBASSY PRESS AND INFORMATION DIVISION

ful crowds kissed their liberators, danced, and celebrated in the streets. They roared a deafening welcome to de Gaulle as he made his triumphant entry into the city. Some Resistance leaders urged him to announce the restoration of the Republic.

"The Republic has never ceased to exist," he said. "Vichy always was and remains null and void. I am the President of the Government of the Republic. Why should I go out and proclaim it?" He simply stepped out on the balcony of the Hotel de Ville to receive the acclamation of millions of ecstatic Parisians roaring, *"Vive de Gaulle!"*

With the reeling Nazi army retreating back into Germany, General Leonard Gerow, American Commander of the Fifth Army Corps, ordered Leclerc's Second Division not to stay in Paris for the victory celebration but to join other Allied forces in hot pursuit of the enemy. De Gaulle was indignant.

"On this day, in this place, such an order indicates a remarkable lack of comprehension," he said in a message to Eisenhower's headquarters. "I lent you General Leclerc. I am taking him back for today!"

The infinitely patient Eisenhower tactfully overruled Gerow, and also withdrew all American forces from Paris so that de Gaulle could mount an all-French victory celebration. Only French troops marched down the Champs Elysées behind de Gaulle in a symbolic ceremony to rekindle the French Eternal Flame at the Arc de Triomphe.

When Eisenhower came to Paris, de Gaulle then insisted that Leclerc's division remain in Paris to support his regime against any possible Communist attempt at a coup. He also demanded that Eisenhower parade the 28th American Division through Paris on their way to the Eastern Front, passing in review before de Gaulle to signify American recognition of him as the interim leader of postwar France.

De Gaulle had barely assumed power in Paris when he began speculating about the role France should play in the postwar world. He visualized his country as holding the balance of power in Europe between East and West.

"I think that in the years ahead, perhaps not so long from now, Russia and America will become rivals for the domination of the world," he told his aide, Maurice Schumann. "This may be dangerous for France, and it may be a great opportunity. We must begin to think what we can do to avert the danger so that France can profit by the opportunity."

He never swerved from that policy decision.

15

Postwar Feuds

AT the end of November, 1944, de Gaulle had gone to Moscow to cultivate Stalin's goodwill. He came home with a treaty of Franco-Soviet friendship that protected him from any coup by Paris Communists, who recognized that Stalin did not want any revolution in France, at least while Hitler was still undefeated. Some Partisans joined de Gaulle's cabinet and accepted seats in the Consultative Assembly.

Communist leaders in the countryside, however, were determined that the Red banner must fly over a liberated France. Armed Partisan units in the southwest took over regions abandoned by the fleeing Germans. But de Gaulle outwitted them by making a personal tour of the liberated provinces. Accepting the acclaim of the French people, he flattered and praised the

Partisans, then proclaimed the freed provinces to be under his new government in Paris.

His success in ending regional Communist revolts, and in putting France solidly behind the final push on Germany, vindicated Eisenhower's support of him in the face of the President's unrelenting opposition. Yet even after the Soviet Union and Britain had recognized the de Gaulle government on October 20th, Roosevelt waited three more days before grudgingly following suit. He and de Gaulle both knew that they would clash stormily over his postwar plans.

"The President," Hull revealed in his *Memoirs*, "favored a four-power establishment that would police the world with the forces of the United States, Britain, Russia and China. All other nations, including France, were to be disarmed."

In December, 1944, Hitler made a last desperate attempt to avoid disaster by his Battle of the Bulge counter-offensive. To shorten Allied supply lines, Eisenhower ordered a strategic retreat from Strasbourg. De Gaulle instantly countermanded the order, telling the French army to fight to hold Strasbourg even if the American forces retired. He was worried that a retreat would shake popular faith in his government's determination not to yield an inch to the Germans.

"Strasbourg is a symbol to the French," he told Eisenhower stubbornly. "I would rather lose the whole French army fighting the Germans to hold it. And I *shall*—if you refuse to commit forces for a last-ditch defense of it!"

"The French army," Eisenhower exploded, "will get no ammunition, supplies or food unless it obeys my orders!"

"If you desert us at Strasbourg, and we are destroyed by the Germans, the wrath of the whole French people will turn

Winston Churchill and Charles de Gaulle reviewing the troops on November 11, 1944.

FRENCH EMBASSY PRESS AND INFORMATION DIVISION

against you. It would mean disaster for our whole cause!"

"But you're asking me to revoke a military order for purely political reasons!"

"Of course!" de Gaulle replied. "Do not armies exist simply to serve the political aims of nations?"

Eisenhower gave in and Strasbourg was held, spared the destruction and massacre a German return would have brought. De Gaulle became a greater hero than ever to the French. At Roosevelt's insistence, however, he was excluded from the Yalta Conference in January, 1945, at which the President, Churchill and Stalin decided the shape of postwar Europe.

De Gaulle was outraged.

"How many Frenchmen, buried in their native land for 2,000 years, must have turned in their grave," he fumed, "when it was known that the fate of vanquished Germany had partly been settled without France having her say!"

He wrote an angry note to the Big Three warning, "The Provisional Government obviously cannot consider itself bound by any of the decisions taken without it."

At the urging of advisers, Roosevelt invited de Gaulle to meet with him aboard his battleship at Algiers, on his way home from Yalta. De Gaulle of course refused. The President then made a disdainful public reference to "a great many prima donnas in the world who wanted to be heard."

De Gaulle was more generous in his appraisal of Roosevelt when the ailing President died on April 12, 1945. "It was with a sincere heart that I tendered his memory my regret and my admiration," he wrote later. In a message of condolence he called Roosevelt "from his first to his last day, the friend of France," and added, "France admired him and loved him."

Yet there was no doubt that the Roosevelt policy toward France and de Gaulle left bitter wounds which would not heal, and served to exacerbate postwar Franco-American relations.

Roosevelt had been a great war leader, generous and idealistic far beyond the egotistic nature of de Gaulle, but he had also had an undeniable blind spot toward the French leader and his nation. De Gaulle had shown a more astute historical perspective and foresight. The two leaders had been almost bound to clash because of their great personal differences—the pragmatic, flexible, informal Roosevelt convinced of his Messianic mission to create a better world order; the rigidly-principled, inflexible, formal de Gaulle, resolved that only Frenchmen could know what was best for France.

Despite Eisenhower's doubts, de Gaulle continued to insist on giving his own orders to French troops to make sure that they redeemed France's honor by taking full part in the final offensive against Germany. Then on May 7, 1945, General de Lattre, head of the French First Army, joined British, Russian and American delegates in witnessing the climax of their common cause—Germany's surrender.

"This is the victory of the United Nations," de Gaulle told the French people. Then in a louder, firmer voice he added emphatically, "*And it is the victory of France!*"

The following day he gave Eisenhower a huge parade in Paris, decorating him under the Arc de Triomphe before millions of cheering Frenchmen. Later, at a French victory dinner in his honor, Eisenhower was called upon for a toast.

"There have been differences—you and I have had some," he said candidly. "But let us bring our troubles to each other

223

On June 14, 1945, Parisians honored General Eisenhower. Here, de Gaulle and Eisenhower after a ceremony at the Arc de Triomphe.

FRENCH EMBASSY PRESS AND INFORMATION DIVISION

Thousands of Parisians jammed the Place de l'Opéra on June 14, 1945, to catch a glimpse of Eisenhower.

FRENCH EMBASSY PRESS AND INFORMATION DIVISION

frankly and face them together. . . . General de Gaulle, I propose to you a toast of friendship—let's be friends!"

De Gaulle's first clash with the new American President, Harry S. Truman, came when the Allied command in Italy sought to take over an area in the Italian Alps held by the French. De Gaulle ordered his troops to resist "with all necessary means." Truman expressed outrage at "the almost unbelievable threat that the French soldiers, bearing American arms, will combat American and Allied soldiers whose efforts and sacrifices have so recently and successfully contributed to the liberation of France itself."

He angrily cut off further military supplies to the French. De Gaulle, realizing that he had gone too far this time, ordered his troops to evacuate the disputed area quietly. But Truman, still angry, refused to lift the ban. De Gaulle flew to Washington to reach an understanding. He got along better with Truman than he had with Roosevelt, but considered the new President to be "very naive" about Europe's problems.

De Gaulle's stubbornness may have made him a thorn in the side of Washington, but it undoubtedly saved France from the second-class status Roosevelt had assigned to it. When Japan capitulated in September, 1945, the Allies bowed to de Gaulle's demand that France be represented among the victors who accepted Japan's surrender. And when the UN Charter was written at San Francisco, France was one of the five "great powers" given permanent seats on the Security Council.

Some American diplomats at the UN expressed concern that France might lead a bloc of the world's small nations against the United States. "Don't worry," French Minister Georges Bidault assured them, "France is too big a country to become the leader of a union to protect small countries."

De Gaulle alone had achieved the incredible restoration of French prestige from its days of defeat, disgrace and occupation only five years earlier, to its status as first-rank world power. He had worked this miracle with only a few exiled followers in London, under sentence of death by Vichy as a traitor, and against the will of the powerful United States. Ironically, it was Roosevelt's stubborn opposition that finally made de Gaulle a hero to the French, who saw him as defying American bullying by refusing to allow Washington to dictate French policy.

When the French electorate voted for a new National Assembly in October, 1945, the legislators unanimously elected de Gaulle as President-Premier. But his halo began to slip as he sought to cope with the realities of a liberated France—shortages of consumer goods and coal, a flourishing black market, spiraling inflation, low wages, antiquated industrial equipment and bitter party rivalries.

His policies proved far too conservative for the Communists and Socialists who dominated the Fourth French Republic. Their combined opposition forced him to resign in January, 1946. He retired to head a new party, the *Mouvemente Republicaine Populaire* (MRP).

The political situation in France was so chaotic that in the first ten postwar years there were no less than twenty different governments, and for a total of 241 days France had no government at all. Without de Gaulle as a rallying point, the French people simply could not agree on any leaders or policies. Every coalition of politicians that managed to form a government quickly became unstuck.

The weakness and instability of the Fourth Republic was reflected in the postwar eruption of France's colonies. In 1946 France was compelled to surrender its mandates over Syria and Lebanon. Its colonial office also agreed to home rule for Indo-China, but then used captured Japanese troops to return southern Vietnam to French colonial control.

"If there is anything that makes my blood boil," General Douglas MacArthur observed angrily from Japan, "it is to see our Allies in Indo-China . . . deploying Japanese troops to re-conquer the little people we promised to liberate. It is the most ignoble kind of betrayal!"

France waged an eight-year colonial war against the nationalist guerrilla forces of Ho Chi Minh, the Communist leader who fought to unite his native Vietnam and make it free not only of France, but also of other great powers who became involved in that struggle—China, Russia and the United States.

Reversing Roosevelt's intention of keeping Indo-China out of French colonial hands, Truman decided to help France hold on to it. His aid program to the colonial French in Saigon was intended to win France as an American ally in the new Cold War struggle between the United States and the Soviet Union for world supremacy and influence. Truman helped keep France herself from going Communist by economic assistance that kept the Fourth Republic afloat until Marshall Plan aid in 1947 strengthened her, along with all of war-weakened Western Europe, against revolution.

Marshall Plan aid helped modernize French industry, whose workers had produced only a third as many goods per man as American labor, and French agriculture, which had produced only a fourth as much food per man as American farmers. The flood of dollars pouring into France also helped to restore coal mines, increase wages, curb prices, and generally stimulate the economy.

"The American aid—which covered all sectors of the economy—continued until 1952," acknowledged the French Ministry of Information, "and helped France to re-establish her war-ruined economy on solid bases, to reconstruct and modernize her equipment." France's gross national product increased an average of ten percent a year.

During this period, when the French government was anxious for Marshall Plan aid to continue, French criticism of American foreign policy was at a minimum. In 1949 the French people sent a "Gratitude Train" through the United States exhibiting the fruits of that aid. The train also displayed their gift to the Brooklyn Museum—a collection of life-sized dolls showing forty-nine changes in French fashions that American women had followed from 1715 to 1906. In April, 1949, France co-operated with American plans for an anti-Soviet European defense system by joining the North Atlantic Treaty Alliance (NATO), despite strong French sentiment for neutrality in the Cold War.

As tensions worsened in that struggle, Secretary of State Dean Acheson increased American aid to France's colonial regime in Saigon. He cited Red Chinese and Soviet support of Ho Chi Minh's Hanoi government in the north as proof that the colonial French fighting Ho were helping to check the forces of international Communism. In February, 1950, Truman recognized a new French puppet government in Saigon headed by former Emperor Bao Dai, an exile and Riviera playboy.

The United States had begun by paying a third of the cost of France's war against Ho, but the American share increased rapidly until it was eighty percent. State Department Far East expert John Ohly warned as early as 1950 that the United States was embarked on a dangerous course in Vietnam, and could be sucked into direct military intervention as the French floundered under Ho's brilliant guerrilla warfare. "These situations have a way of snowballing," he observed.

"While we may have tried to muddle through and were certainly not successful," Acheson admitted later, "I could not think then or later of a better course. One can suggest, perhaps, doing nothing. That might have had merit, but . . . it had its demerits, too."

As the French position in Vietnam worsened, French generals made frequent trips to Washington to demand more American aid. They were indignant when Acheson questioned their political strategy. "At this time," he recalled, "we began an effort—a frustrating and unsuccessful one—to get our friends to see and face the facts in Indo-China. France was engaged in a task beyond her strength."

He tried to persuade the French colonialists that the only way to win popular support against Communism in Indo-China was by agreeing to real independence for the Saigon regime, Laos and Cambodia, but they turned deaf ears.

Meanwhile a familiar American face had returned to France to head NATO—General Dwight D. Eisenhower. When he appeared at a performance of the *Comédie Française* in the box of the President of France, the entire audience rose to its feet to cheer and applaud the war hero who had liberated them from Nazi tyranny seven years earlier. Eisenhower had not forgotten either. He visited the American cemetery above Omaha Beach, staring down at the rotting hulks and half-buried emergency docks, remembering the spectacle of ships and troops as far as the eye could see.

The French Communist press now pictured him as a cruel military despot trying to drag Europe into another war. But the non-Communist French press wittily embarrassed their Paris comrades by reprinting the 1944 editorials in which the Communists had hailed Eisenhower as "the great Liberator."

De Gaulle waited for Eisenhower to call on him, but the head of NATO carefully kept his distance. He knew that de Gaulle wanted France, not the United States, to dominate any European alliance. De Gaulle also vehemently opposed the American plan to bring her traditional foe, West Germany, into NATO.

France was sliding into deep trouble because of her costly, futile war in Vietnam; demands by French Morocco for independence; and a decline in the value of the franc. Many French agreed with the Communist press, blaming American foreign policy for France's difficulties.

The French also deplored the wave of irrational anti-Communist hysteria sweeping the United States under the aegis of Senator Joseph McCarthy. Huge crowds in Paris demonstrated against the execution of Julius and Ethel Rosenberg, Americans convicted of being Soviet spies.

"Watch out—America has the rabies!" Jean-Paul Sartre told his countrymen the day after the Rosenbergs were put to death. "Cut all ties which bind us to her, otherwise we will in turn be bitten and run mad!"

The French government complained to the State Depart-

Jean-Paul Sartre, the great French philosopher and exponent of existentialism.

FRENCH EMBASSY PRESS AND INFORMATION DIVISION

ment over the American failure to support French colonialism in North Africa, despite the U.S. air bases allowed to operate there. Acheson related, "I encouraged all our French friends to speak at length, holding nothing back. They fully enjoyed complying and disclosed . . . a good deal of pent-up resentment."

He assured the French that their fear that the Americans were attempting to replace French influence in Africa was unfounded. The heart of the matter, he explained, was simply a traditional American sympathy for all oppressed colonial peoples—an explanation that rang hollow even in the days before Vietnam. Understandably, French distrust of U.S. foreign policy increased.

After Eisenhower became President in 1953, control of American foreign policy passed into the hands of Secretary of State John Foster Dulles. A rigid anti-Communist, intolerant of any nation that did not align itself completely with American policies, Dulles told the balky French that, like it or not, the German army would be built up in NATO as the most powerful force of the European army.

Dulles believed in a "domino theory," that is, if Ho Chi Minh's Communist regime were allowed to triumph in Vietnam over French colonialism, it would "topple the other dominos" of Indo-China, one after the other, into the Communist camp. He increased the amount of aid to the French in Saigon, but was unable to prevent their crucial defeat at Dienbienphu by Ho and General Vo Nguyen Giap.

The French generals called for direct American military intervention to save their crumbling colonial empire in Southeast Asia. Dulles wanted to go to their rescue with bombing raids, using nuclear weapons if necessary. Vice-President Richard Nixon urged the commitment of U.S. ground forces to Vietnam. Both were prudently overruled by President Eisenhower, who was aware that such intervention would be deplored not only by most Americans, but also by all of America's allies. Britain's Anthony Eden reminded Eisenhower that if he became bogged down in a land war in Asia, the Soviet Union would be left free to make strategic countermoves elsewhere.

The President declared that he could not "conceive of a greater tragedy for America than to get involved now in an all-out war in any of those regions."

When Dienbienphu fell in May, 1954, the French decided that there was no further point in trying to pursue the war that was causing bankruptcy in France and was polarizing the nation. They asked for a peace conference at Geneva.

Supported by nineteen nations, the Geneva Accords ended the fighting in Vietnam by temporarily dividing the country into two zones. One was governed by Ho Chi Minh in the North; the other was under temporary French control in the South, until elections scheduled within two years produced an independent government for all of Vietnam. It was generally conceded, even by Eisenhower, that Ho would win at least eighty percent of the popular vote.

The international settlement at Geneva displeased Dulles. Although agreeing to do nothing to upset the Accords, he refused to sign them, and effectively sabotaged them by establishing Ngo Dinh Diem as puppet dictator of the Saigon regime, and by supplying him with arms and funds.

Diem's assignment was to wreck the Accords by keeping the country divided permanently into North and South "nations," and preventing the scheduled elections in 1956. Diem fulfilled these tasks. Through its support of him, the United States became more and more deeply committed to the tragic Vietnam War that raged on through the administrations of Kennedy, Johnson and Nixon, creating an American protest movement that plunged the country into national crisis.

When France emerged from the Geneva Accords, however, Vietnam was no longer a drain on her resources, manpower and national unity, and her commercial interests in South Vietnam were profitably intact. The French were incredulous that the Americans, after having seen France trapped in the quicksands of Southeast Asia, nevertheless plunged ahead to repeat the same catastrophic mistakes.

When Charles de Gaulle later visited the White House in 1961, he warned its new occupant, John F. Kennedy, that the United States would meet disaster in Indo-China if it persisted in sabotaging the Geneva Accords. "I predict you will gradually slide into a bottomless military and political quagmire, despite the losses and expenses you will lavish," de Gaulle said. He later wrote in his memoirs, "Kennedy listens. But events will show that I have not convinced him."

16

France Goes Her Own Way

ALTHOUGH the French colonialists had taken a drubbing at Dienbienphu in 1954, they had not been cured of their thirst for new colonial adventures. In 1956, when Egypt's anti-colonial Gamal Abdel Nasser seized the Suez Canal, France joined Britain and Israel in secretly mobilizing an invasion force that attacked Egypt to overthrow him. Through the UN, President Eisenhower forced all three nations to withdraw their forces. "There can be no law," he insisted, "if we invoke one code of international conduct for those we oppose, and another for our friends."

In 1958, French colonial generals in Algiers, fearful that the government in Paris was going to conciliate Algerian rebel nationalists, staged a revolt. They demanded a recall to power of Charles de Gaulle, threatening otherwise to invade France with paratroops. But de Gaulle refused to return to office.

Finally he was offered special powers as President of a more authoritarian Fifth Republic.

Demonstrating both courage and foresight, he liquidated the now uncontrollable French Empire. The Algerian generals were dismayed when he ended the French North African conflict by awarding independence to Algeria four years later. De Gaulle's real interests lay in Europe. Pursuing his old dream of restoring France to her ancient glory as a great power on the continent, he was determined to end both France's dependence on the United States and American influence in Europe.

He called for a detente with the Russians and an end to the sterile Cold War that divided Europe, seeking to unite the continent under French leadership as a neutral force between the two nuclear giants. Much to the dismay of President Eisenhower, in 1959 he withdrew part of the French fleet in the Mediterranean, as well as some of France's ground forces, from the NATO command. France, he declared, could no longer handcuff her full military power to NATO and have no control of it for her own needs.

He spelled out new demands for continued French participation in the Atlantic Alliance: France must now be given an equal voice with the United States and Britain in deciding Western global strategy. The French must also be allowed to manufacture their own nuclear weapons, instead of being forced to rely on America's "nuclear umbrella." President Eisenhower rejected these demands, even though as France's wartime liberator he had often sympathized with de Gaulle's proud insistence upon French self-determination.

De Gaulle promptly ordered American nuclear stockpiles

removed from French territory unless they were transferred to French control. It was "intolerable for a great state," he declared, to allow its basic security to rest upon the whim of another nation, no matter how friendly. So in 1959 the United States was forced to dismantle some American bases in France and remove them to West Germany or Britain. De Gaulle then began developing France's own nuclear weapons.

"The Russians now have long-range weapons," he explained. "If one of their explosives were to fall on France, Washington would not go to war immediately. It would only fight immediately if a bomb fell on the United States. Thus France is not defended by NATO, and NATO prevents France from serving her own interests. France must take back its independence. NATO is no longer an alliance, it is a subordination. We cannot [allow] a superior, like the United States, to be responsible for us."

Washington was further angered when de Gaulle's blackball kept Britain out of the Common Market, a trading alliance of six European nations. De Gaulle viewed the British as a "Trojan horse" for American interests. But he was equally wary of the Russian bear hug. When Soviet Premier Nikita Khrushchev came to Paris in 1960 to woo de Gaulle into a Soviet military alliance, he met with a courteous but firm rebuff. To emphasize France's neutrality, de Gaulle made an official visit to Washington afterward.

Eisenhower received him warmly, and they discussed an important four-power summit meeting to be held in Paris to end the Cold War. This time de Gaulle would be one of the Big Four leaders participating.

Just before the summit meeting opened in May, the Russians shot down a high-flying American U-2 spy plane deep inside Soviet territory. When the Big Four convened in Paris, Khrushchev broke into a blistering tirade against Eisenhower, demanding a public apology. The embarrassed President was grateful for the cool, dignified way in which de Gaulle came to his defense. Frustrated by de Gaulle's refusal to support the Soviet position, Khrushchev stormed out of the Conference.

"General de Gaulle's emergence as the leader of the West . . . was far from the least important result of the explosion at the Summit," reported columnist Joseph Alsop from Paris. "A much greater debt is owed to the French President than most people understand. His untroubled perception and icy imperturbability in a moment of potential danger prevented an even uglier result in Paris."

Baffled American critics who saw de Gaulle only as an anti-American, anti-democratic dictator were dumbfounded when he voluntarily gave independence to no less than fourteen former French colonies in Africa in 1960. Many, but not all, chose to join an economic French Union.

De Gaulle again came to the defense of the United States in the fall of 1962 when it clashed with the Soviet Union over the Russian installation of nuclear missiles in Castro's Cuba. De Gaulle voiced support of the American position in establishing a naval blockade of Cuba, defying Khrushchev until the Russian leader agreed to remove the missiles.

But once the crisis was over, de Gaulle did not hesitate to point out the correctness of his own position in divorcing France from American policy, since Washington was obviously ready to risk nuclear war involving all the allies in NATO without first consulting with them.

239

He speeded up France's own nuclear program, convinced that as a nuclear power France could replace the United States as the leader of Europe. When the Americans, British and Russians signed a limited Nuclear Test Ban Treaty in 1963, de Gaulle joined Red China in refusing to sign it. Despite his differences with Washington, de Gaulle insisted that they in no way changed France's close ties with the United States.

"For us, the fundamental assumption of French-American relations is friendship and alliance," he declared in July, 1963. "For almost two hundred years that friendship has existed as an eminent psychological reality, basic to the nature of the two countries. . . . The friendship which unites them and the alliance which binds them are unassailable."

Ignoring Washington's boycott of Red China, he recognized Mao's government in 1964. He scoffed at the American puppet regime in Saigon and called for its replacement by a neutral government to end the Vietnam War. And he persisted in his opposition to NATO by refusing to attend its twentieth anniversary celebration of D-Day.

De Gaulle kept French public opinion solidly behind him by controlling France's television programs. He watched television for two hours every night to make sure that the news and documentaries justified his policies by showing the United States in an unflattering light, with emphasis on Vietnam and race riots.

"How can you govern a country," his Minister of Culture, Andre Malraux, asked an American diplomat dryly, "in which the government doesn't control the television programs?"

Another spokesman for French television pointed out that French commentators were "certainly no more aggressive than

240

anti-French commentators heard occasionally on American networks." He added, "Franco-American relations are going through a critical time. . . . I hope that the friendship existing between our two countries is strong enough to bear with these temporary difficulties."

In the brief years that Kennedy was in the White House, Franco-American relations were at their least rancorous. De Gaulle admired the young President, his attractive, French-speaking wife, and Sargent Shriver, Kennedy's brother-in-law, who became a popular Ambassador to France. De Gaulle was contemptuous, however, of Kennedy's Texan Vice President, Lyndon Johnson.

When Johnson visited Paris, de Gaulle asked him superciliously, "Well, Mr. Vice President, what have you come to Paris to learn?" Stung, Johnson retorted, "Why, General, anything you *think* you can teach me!"

After Kennedy's assassination put Johnson in the White House, Franco-American relations cooled sharply. Johnson regarded de Gaulle with a mixture of impatience and dislike, and did not bother to conceal his feelings.

At a diplomatic luncheon he compared de Gaulle to "a grouchy old grandfather grumbling by the stove." He told the gathering, "De Gaulle is like a train that scatters people walking on the track. But as soon as the train has passed I am back again with my friend [West German Chancellor] Erhard walking arm in arm down the same track."

These public remarks brought this response from de Gaulle:

"There is no hate for the United States in France. France remains friendly to the United States, but the French people don't like the American people. The United States is our

241

friend and will remain so, but the American people are not regarded sympathetically. From time to time when moments of great danger arise, then only the United States and France will remain, and people will tend to forget 'the Americans' and 'the French' who do not get on so well. Of course, during intervening periods, the fact that our interests are not really the same will continue to appear."

Writing from Paris in 1965, C.L. Sulzberger agreed in *The New York Times:* "The French and the Americans often display an unhappy talent for misunderstanding and irritating each other. . . . Whether France and the United States or Frenchmen and Americans love each other doesn't really matter. We are friends and we should remain allies." But in 1966 de Gaulle announced an almost total French withdrawal from NATO. In 1967, NATO headquarters were moved from Paris to Belgium.

In July of that year de Gaulle created a furore on the American continent during a state visit to Canada. In a speech at Montreal, he encouraged the French separatist movement in Quebec by crying out, "Long live Free Quebec!" The Canadian government was stunned at what sounded almost like a French bid to retake French-speaking Quebec for the old French Empire in North America. De Gaulle was bluntly rebuked for his unprecedented violation of protocol. He defiantly asserted that France would aid the people of Quebec in attaining "the objectives of liberation that they themselves have set." His encouragement unquestionably helped set the scene three years later for the violence into which the revolutionary wing of the Quebec Liberation Front plunged Canada.

The press in the United States was indignant at de Gaulle's

*President Kennedy and General de Gaulle at the Elysée Palace
on May 31, 1961.*

FRENCH EMBASSY PRESS AND INFORMATION DIVISION

interference in North American affairs. One commentator suggested that the Prime Minister of Canada ought to make a state visit to France to whip up revolt in Britany, where Bretons for generations had been struggling to separate themselves from France.

When Georges Pompidou later succeeded de Gaulle, he was compelled to observe, "Jacques Cartier is dead and so is Montcalm; we do not intend to annex Quebec. It is nonetheless true that we cannot fail to have very close and even friendly relations with the French people in Quebec, for reasons of history, race, language and culture."

To dispel grumbling in the American press that the French had short memories of what they owed to Americans, French Ambassador Charles Lucet assured the Women's National Democratic Club in Washington in October, 1967, "We are grateful to those who . . . enabled us to recover our prosperity and to preserve our independence. I am thinking of course of you, our American friends, and we know what the Marshall Plan did for us."

De Gaulle was more ambivalent at a farewell dinner in Paris he gave for American Ambassador Charles E. Bohlen in January, 1968: "Perhaps this friendship may appear to be undergoing some difficulties at the present. But during its history, which is nearly two hundred years old now, it is not the first time. For it certainly seems that there is always one of our two countries whose instinct inclines it to moderation when the other tends to abandon moderation.

"At the various times when France was choosing to lead a hazardous life, she did not unfailingly have the United States' support. Today, when the latter in its turn is particularly susceptible to the impulses of power, it is true that France does not always approve it."

So little did de Gaulle approve, in fact, that his foreign policy was largely based on reducing American power around the world. He entered negotiations for military, space and nuclear research agreements with the Soviet Union. Turning over $90 million in American dollar credits to Algeria, he specified that they were to be redeemed for gold, in order to weaken the U.S. dollar and drive down its value. France's client state of Gabon in West Africa was pressured to expel fifty-seven Peace Corps workers as suspected CIA agents. Prince Sihanouk was supported in his protests against American intervention in then neutral Cambodia.

De Gaulle's feud with American "imperialism" created a backlash of indignation in the United States. Many Americans began to boycott French clothes, textiles and wines. Senator George Smathers indignantly demanded imposition of a head tax of $250 on every American tourist traveling to France. Senator Henry Jackson attacked de Gaulle as "a senile individual the U.S. can no longer tolerate." Washington refused to sell France any more enriched uranium, and discouraged American business interests from investing in French industry.

The French press reported these developments as proof that Washington was guilty of waging aggressive economic warfare—the same Washington, Frenchmen were reminded, that had once coddled Vichy France, snubbed de Gaulle and heaped contempt on France as a third-rate nation.

Some political observers were convinced that the roots of the Franco-American feud were to be found less in basic political disagreements than in de Gaulle's long-smoldering resentment over his shabby and short-sighted treatment by Roosevelt during World War II.

De Gaulle's vendetta, if that's what it was, was not without support in the rest of Europe, where American arrogance was often resented as much as American help was appreciated. "Do not many of us secretly share de Gaulle's pleasure in humiliating the Americans?" asked the London *Sunday Telegraph*. "The truth is that the general is a much more representative figure than we like to think."

Critical as he was of Johnson's escalation of the war in Vietnam, de Gaulle gave him credit when he finally announced a bombing halt in 1968. "For the President of the United States . . . [it] seems to be a first step in the direction of peace," the French leader observed, "and consequently an act of reason and political courage." Significantly, Paris was the site that both sides agreed upon for peace talks.

Like Johnson, de Gaulle neglected serious domestic problems in his absorption with foreign affairs. Both France and the U.S. were racked with violent and huge protest demonstrations. De Gaulle solved his crisis temporarily by pledging thorough-going reforms of French society.

Jean-Jacques Servan-Shreiber, anti-Gaullist editor of the Paris *L'Express*, told *Life* magazine's American readers: "The students and workers of France do not accept the American society, either, because they think it is a cruel and unjust one, albeit modern. We must invent a society that is not the Soviet one, and that is not the American one."

Michel Debré, de Gaulle's Foreign Minister, visited Washington in October, 1968, in an effort to prevent the Franco-American feud from worsening. The causes, he believed, were chiefly French condemnation of the American role in Vietnam, and American resentment of France's independent foreign policy. After his visit he declared that he believed Washington was beginning to accept the French point of view.

By January, 1969, French Ambassador Charles Lucet could tell an American audience, "It seems to me that after a period of nervousness . . . things have come back to normal between us, or almost so. . . . A new conception of our traditional friendship is gradually coming to light. . . . One's best friend is not always he who endorses one's decisions in advance, and who refuses to think because he needs Washington's immediate support."

When Richard M. Nixon became President, he visited Paris and afterwards declared, "General de Gaulle believes that Europe should have an increasingly independent position in its own right, and frankly I believe that too."

In April, 1969, de Gaulle held a referendum seeking a vote of confidence from the French people. To his shock he lost. The practical French people had decided that the grandeur de Gaulle had returned to France did not compensate for poor roads, a low standard of living, badly overcrowded schools and the suffering of millions of small tradesmen caught between high taxes and proliferating supermarkets. De Gaulle promptly resigned and retired in proud seclusion, an unquestionably great French leader who had left an indelible imprint on Franco-American relations.

His successor, Georges Pompidou, declared in his first press conference in July, 1969, "The conversations that President Nixon and General de Gaulle had in Paris have marked a turning point, or in any case, brought things back to their right

President Nixon and General de Gaulle, 1969.
FRENCH EMBASSY PRESS AND INFORMATION DIVISION

proportions. The United States and France cannot have the same view on everything, for obvious reasons, but the two chiefs of state were able to note that . . . the goals were close to each other, if not common."

Pompidou reiterated that France would remain "not only the friend of the United States, but its ally, "despite their differences over NATO. He also thought that Nixon's promise to wind down the war in Vietnam "should make it possible to wipe out the last clouds . . . between us."

In late February, 1970, Pompidou made a state visit to the United States at the invitation of Nixon. He and his wife ran into furious anti-French demonstrations by large crowds of pro-Israeli Americans who were angered by the French sale of jet fighter planes to the Arabs. Insulted and jostled during a tour of several cities, Pompidou complained to Nixon. He denounced the anti-French demonstrations as "a stain on the forehead of America," and revealed that his wife, greatly upset, was returning at once to France. The President hastily phoned the Pompidous in New York to apologize.

Attending a farewell banquet for them there, Nixon said, "When I learned that President and Madame Pompidou were coming to the United States, I wanted them to see our country . . . as a President of the United States saw it. And I must say, we overdid it a bit, as we usually do." When the laughter subsided, he added, "Our friendship is so deep and so long that any minor irritation or bad manners or differences are not going to impair it. . . . I am proud tonight to say goodbye to the President of France as a personal friend."

Invited to address a joint session of Congress, Pompidou declared, "Liberty, peace, cooperation. These are the ideals we share. These are what closely unite us . . . [even when] there are times where immediate interests prevail."

The Russian press saw the Pompidous' stormy American reception as having been secretly encouraged by the White House, in order to impress the French with American displeasure over France's treaty negotiations with Moscow; French opposition to the Vietnam War; French withdrawal from NATO; and French opposition to American policies in the Middle East.

"American Zionists," observed Soviet columnist Nikolai Borodin, "haven't yet blown up the Statue of Liberty—a present from the people of France—but after their noisy demonstrations against President Pompidou you can expect anything. . . . The anti-French demonstrations in America were engineered by the Zionists with the complete connivance and blessing of the U.S. authorities."

When Nixon decided to invade Cambodia with American troops in May, 1970, Pompidou indicated his disapproval to the American Embassy in Paris. "There will be prospects for peace in Indo-China only when the United States has taken by itself, and voluntarily, the firm resolution to evacuate Indo-China," he said. "That is the basis of everything. . . . May these unfortunate peoples no longer be made the subject and the victim of rivalries which . . . do not even concern them. That is France's policy." He said nothing about the same wrong policies France had followed in Indo-China fifteen years earlier.

Despite such friction, there was harmonious Franco-American co-operation on such non-political problems as drug addiction. During Pompidou's visit Nixon asked him for a crackdown on French drug smugglers. In July, 1970, the U.S. Bureau on Narcotics and Dangerous Drugs credited the French *Sureté* with excellent co-operation in curbing this traffic.

The death of de Gaulle in November, 1970, brought Nixon to Paris to attend the funeral of France's greatest modern figure, who had once said of himself, "De Gaulle is not Left, Right or Center—de Gaulle is *above*." In his memoirs de Gaulle wrote, "All my life I have thought of France . . . as dedicated to an exalted and exceptional destiny. . . . France cannot be France without greatness."

Pompidou declared, "General de Gaulle is dead. France is a widow. In 1940 General de Gaulle saved our honor, in 1944 he led us to liberty and victory. In 1958 he averted civil war. He gave modern France her institutions, her independence and her place in the world."

Although the United States had often considered him, in Secretary of State Dean Rusk's phrase, "a boulder in the stream of history," Stewart Alsop wrote in *Newsweek*, "De Gaulle's purpose . . . to the day of his death, was to restore the shattered self-respect of the defeated French . . . to rebuild their pride in France as a great nation."

And no one could deny that he had.

17
Our Exasperating Friends

FOLLOWING Pompidou's visit to the United States, the French Institute of Public Opinion took a poll to find out how the French people felt about the bittersweet relations between the two countries. It reported fifty-nine percent satisfied, and the rest either dissatisfied or undecided. Some twenty-nine percent named the United States as France's best friend, a finding the French government offered as proof of French affection for Americans, ignoring the fact that seventy-one percent of the French people thought otherwise. Although, since no other country got more than a ten percent vote as France's best friend, perhaps that distinction did, indeed, belong to the United States.

A few years earlier, however, anti-American feeling had been so pronounced in France that American tourists widely complained of being snarled at, mistreated and overcharged by French cab drivers, waiters, hotel personnel and shopkeepers. Many American travelers began to leave France off their vacation itineraries.

Worried about the loss of tourist income, as well as damage to France's reputation as a vacationland, the French Minister of Tourism organized a "National Amiability Campaign." Americans were welcomed at the airport with a rose, and given books of "smile checks" to be distributed to courteous French service personnel. The checks were redeemed at the Ministry of Tourism by Frenchmen willing to be pleasant to even American tourists for a suitable cash reward.

"The idea of amiability being organized by the Ministry of Tourism," laughed columnist Jean-Francois Revel in the French newspaper *L'Express*, "is more ridiculous than offensive." That it was considered necessary by the government, however, was in itself a commentary on French feelings about Americans in recent decades.

On the other hand, American tourists themselves were not blameless. Many were arrogantly patronizing in their dealings with the French. Too often the complexity and subtlety of French behavior was lost on the more simplistic Americans. The French are an ironic, vivacious and egalitarian people who are invariably stimulating company. But their reactions are confusing because they often respond to emotions by analyzing them intellectually, and to ideas by reacting to them emotionally.

"Most of them can't even speak English!" grumbled a lady tourist from Wisconsin who spoke no French. Such insensitive provincialism understandably aroused resentment among the French.

The situation may have improved. An American Embassy attaché in Paris reported that a favorable impression of Americans is being spread by many Frenchmen returning from visits to the United States. Besides, prosperous German tourists flooding Paris were rapidly replacing Americans as the chief targets of intense French hostility.

The view of the French held by the majority of Americans still tends to reflect Protestant suspicions of a Catholic nation and puritanical suspicions of French "immorality." Americans have traditionally regarded the French as a sensual, irreligious, frivolous people. How could the United States take seriously or trust a volatile, decadent people absorbed in fashions, millinery, painting, dancing and love-making?

Only a relatively small number of American intellectuals, scientists and creative people has understood and appreciated the great intellectual and artistic accomplishments of the French, and their important influence on American culture. The American middle class has often swayed back and forth between the two extreme views, or has sought to merge them, resulting in a confusing composite image of the French.

Even so jingoistic an American as Theodore Roosevelt, after a lecture tour of France, was forced to admit, "It shows my own complacent Anglo-Saxon ignorance that I had hitherto rather looked down upon French public men. . . . When I met them I found that they had just as solid characters as English and American public men . . . with the attractiveness which to my mind makes the able and cultivated Frenchman really unique."

If the French have influenced American cultural standards, America has unquestionably influenced French living patterns.

Janet Flanner, Paris correspondent for *The New Yorker*, reported during the Sixties, "Paris has become Americanized. All France, through its big cities, has become Americanized. Oddly enough, we Americans were at first very popular because of what the French wanted from us—our twentieth century. Now they are taking our language, our slang and business jargon and have inserted it into their own language. The mixture is called Franglais. Which began with the French saying, *Très bien*, O.K. Snack bars, supermarkets, cafeterias and hot dogs are a few of the gustatory contributions of America to modern France."

Every year thousands of American college juniors elect to take their third year's study in Paris, as much to enjoy France as to advance their education. Many report finding the French highly critical, not only of American policy in Vietnam and the treatment of minorities, but also of what they regard as the low level of American culture.

The reason the French dislike Americans and are rude to them, explained General Pierre Billotte, Chairman of a French Assembly committee on Franco-American friendship, is that "France has an inferiority complex. You must know this and expect it to be expressed in aggressiveness."

In Fodor's *Guide to France*, George Mikes insists that Americans can nevertheless find plenty of old-fashioned courtesy outside of Paris. "Like New Yorkers, Parisians are often busy, hurried and nervous," he explains. "The further one goes from the central tourist sections, the nicer, politer, and more helpful they are likely to be."

Most Americans who visit France, former Premier André Tardieu once complained, "carry back only the most super-

255

Bouquinistes (*secondhand book dealers*) *along the Left Bank of the Seine. In the background is Notre Dame.*

FRENCH CULTURAL SERVICES

ficial impressions about French life, gained in places where French people never set their feet. . . . The size of the American colony and the swarms of American tourists keep them in purely American surroundings. Most of them see us from the outside looking in. . . . Of the whole world, the United States . . . is probably the least well-informed about France."

It is certainly possible to live in Paris and still remain sealed within an American environment. Paris has an American Library, a United States House, an American Students' and Artists' Center, an American Chamber of Commerce, an American University Union, an American Club, an Association of American University Women, an American Aid Society, and an American Hospital.

Tardieu charged that Americans tend to judge the French without appreciating that for fifteen centuries France, unlike the United States, had frontiers to defend and was constantly forced to repel invaders by land and sea.

"If they were more human, more modest, and better informed," he wrote, "Americans would . . . refrain from many of the unjust . . . insults to which France has been subjected." He accused Washington of an overbearing brand of diplomacy that made international co-operation difficult, and of blaming other countries for balkiness. "The United States herself would seem to have been always most to blame," he insisted.

But Tardieu also admitted that French ignorance about Americans was equally "unbelievable." Nine out of ten Frenchmen, he declared, believed that Congress elected the American President. "If better days are to be hoped for, mutual enlightenment must be organized . . . for it does not exist," he

These two Frenchmen were left without work when les Halles, the famous open air markets of Paris, were reestablished in Rungis in 1969.

FRENCH CULTURAL SERVICES

warned. "Of what worth is the teaching in American history that French youth receives? Nothing, less than nothing, for it contains the germs of all the habitual and poisonous errors. . . . Is young America any better informed about France? It does not seem so."

He was a strong advocate of student exchanges, pointing out, "We have seen young Americans, chosen by merit, coming to France for brief visits which taught them better than any books could have done something of the real France." He also praised the value of tours of the United States arranged for French students, and of professor exchanges.

"Only our wine-growers have been able, by much patient labor, to mate lastingly the soil of France with American vines," said Tardieu. "It is our duty to imitate them."

Despite their frequent quarrels, Americans and the French have usually felt bound together, as history has shown since 1776, in a profound common cause. The Americans expressed it as "life, liberty and the pursuit of happiness," the French as *"liberté, egalité et fraternité."*

But when not fighting side by side against common enemies for the defense of these treasured principles, they have undeniably found each other mutually exasperating.

"Do not try to understand the French," dryly advises George Mikes. "They are . . . much too complicated and European for the Americans. . . . The French have always been clear in their minds as to what they want, and they have hardly ever gotten what they wanted. A century and a half ago they wanted a Jacobin revolution and they got a national empire. . . . The French are the most misunderstood people in the world. . . . Americans seem never to have looked at the map and do not realize that while it keeps changing, France is always left just on the western edge of whatever danger threatens."

Few Americans appreciate that the French, in seeking to create a united Europe for Europeans, independent of American influence and control, are actually paying a supreme compliment to the American form of government.

Perhaps one day the American people will even help our exasperating friends, the French, to realize this dream by supporting their aspirations for a free, strong and independent United States of Europe.

Bibliography and Suggested Reading

Suggested further reading indicated by (*)

ACHESON, DEAN.
    Present at the Creation. New York: W. W. Norton & Company, Inc., 1969.

AMBASSADE DE FRANCE.
    The Bonaparte Family and the United States. New York: Service de Presse et d'Information, 1969.

APPEL, BENJAMIN.
    With Many Voices. New York: William Morrow and Company, 1963.

* ——. *France and America.* New York: Service de Presse et d'Information, undated.

* ARCHER, JULES.
    Battlefield President: Dwight D. Eisenhower. New York: Julian Messner, 1967.

* ——. *The Extremists.* New York: Hawthorn Books, Inc., Publishers, 1969.

——. *Fighting Journalist: Horace Greeley.* New York: Julian Messner, 1966.

——. *Front-Line General: Douglas MacArthur.* New York: Julian Messner, 1963.

* ———. *The Unpopular Ones.* New York: Crowell-Collier Press. London: Collier-Macmillan Limited, 1968.

* ———. *World Citizen: Woodrow Wilson.* New York: Julian Messner, 1967.

* ASBURY, HERBERT.
   The French Quarter. New York: Alfred A. Knopf, 1936.

AYLING, S. E.
   Portraits of Power. New York: Barnes & Noble, Inc., Publishers, 1963.

* BAINBRIDGE, JOHN.
   Another Way of Living. New York, Chicago, San Francisco: Holt, Rinehart and Winston, 1968.

BRINTON, CRANE.
   The Americans and the French. Cambridge, Mass.: Harvard University Press, 1968.

* DE GRAMONT, SANCHE.
   The French. New York: G. P. Putnam's Sons, 1969.

ERGANG, ROBERT.
   Europe Since Waterloo. Boston: D. C. Heath and Company, 1961.

FODOR, EUGENE.
   France 1970. New York: David McKay Company, Inc., 1970.

FURNAS, J. C.
   The Americans. New York: G. P. Putnam's Sons, 1969.

GRINNELL-MILNE, DUNCAN.
> *The Triumph of Integrity*. New York: The Macmillan
> Company, 1962.

HADLEY, ARTHUR T.
> *Power's Human Face*. New York: William Morrow &
> Company, 1965.

HATCH, ALDEN.
> *The de Gaulle Nobody Knows*. New York: Hawthorn
> Books, Inc., Publishers, 1960.

JONES, HOWARD MUMFORD.
> *America and French Culture*. Chapel Hill, N.C.: The
> University of North Carolina Press, 1927.

JOSEPH, FRANZ M., ED.
> *As Others See Us*. Princeton, N.J.: Princeton University
> Press, 1959.

LONG, DAVID F.
> *The Outward View*. Chicago, New York, San Francisco:
> Rand McNally & Company, 1963.

MAUROIS, ANDRÉ.
> *The Miracle of America*. New York and London: Harper
> & Brothers Publishers, 1944.

* MCKAY, DONALD C.
> *The United States and France*. Cambridge, Mass.: Har-
> vard University Press, 1951.

MONTGOMERY, D. H.
> *American History*. Boston: Ginn & Company, Publishers,
> 1893.

264

NICHOLS, ROY F.
American Leviathan. New York: Harper & Row, Publishers, 1963.

* PADOVER, SAUL K.
Jefferson. New York: The New American Library, 1952.
PARKMAN, FRANCIS.
Pioneers of France in the New World. Boston: Little, Brown & Company, 1867.
* PIERSON, GEORGE WILSON.
Tocqueville In America. Garden City, New York: Doubleday & Company, Inc., 1959.

SENATE REPUBLICAN POLICY COMMITTEE.
The War in Vietnam. Washington, D.C.: Public Affairs Press, 1967.
SIEGFRIED, ANDRÉ.
America At Mid-Century. New York: Harcourt, Brace and Company, 1955.
SNYDER, LOUIS L. AND RICHARD B. MORRIS.
They Saw It Happen. Harrisburg, Pa.: The Stackpole Company, 1951.
STROUT, CUSHING.
The American Image of the Old World. New York, Evanston, and London: Harper & Row, Publishers, 1963.

* TARDIEU, ANDRÉ.
France and America. Boston and New York: Houghton Mifflin Company, 1927.

TOURNOUX, JEAN-RAYMOND.
   Sons of France. New York: The Viking Press, 1964.

* VIORST, MILTON.
   Hostile Allies: FDR and de Gaulle. New York: The Macmillan Company. London: Collier-Macmillan Ltd., 1965.

* WHITE, ELIZABETH BRETT.
   American Opinion of France. New York: Alfred A. Knopf, 1927.
WICKES, GEORGE.
   Americans In Paris. Garden City, New York: Doubleday & Company, Inc., 1969.
WILLIAMS, GWYN A.
   Artisans and Sans-Culottes. New York: W. W. Norton & Company, Inc., 1969.

Articles and news stories on Franco-American relations consulted for this book were found in *Ambassade de France* news releases, *American History Illustrated, Life, Mankind, The Nation, The New Republic, Newsweek, The New York Times, The New York Times Magazine, The New Yorker,* the *New York Post, The Soviet Weekly, Time* and *TV Guide.*

Index

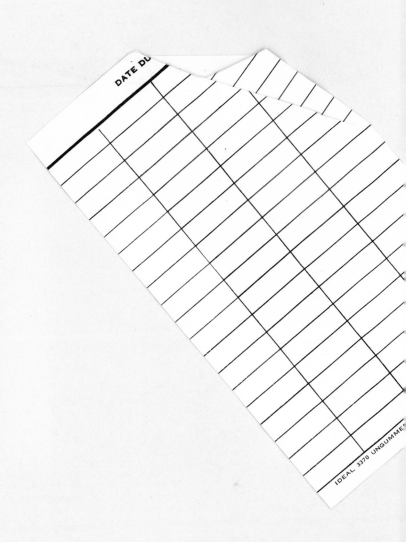

DATE DUE

IDEAL 3370 UNGUMMED